Dear Self, Please Forgive Me

A Woman's Guide to Self-Love and Forgiveness

T.L. Johnson

Ashley, may your heart be blessed with the words from my heart and soul. You are more than enough. Live, Love, & Be FREE!

Copyright © 2020 Tracie Johnson

All rights reserved. No parts of this book may be reproduced, stored, or transmitted by any means- whether auditory, graphic, mechanical, or electronic- without written permission of both publisher and author, except in the case of brief excerpts used in critical articles and reviews. Unauthorized reproduction of any part of this work is illegal and is punishable by law.

ISBN-13: 979-8-674-53209-5

Library of Congress Control Number: 2020917910

Imprint: Independently published

For more information, please visit:
www.traciejohnson.com
www.livelovebefree.com
Instagram:pennedbytracie

Because of the dynamic nature of the internet, any web addresses or links contained in this book may have changed since publication and may no longer be valid. The views expressed in this work are solely those of the author and do not necessarily reflect the views of the publisher, and the publisher disclaims any responsibility for them.

Any people depicted in stock imagery are models, and such images are being used for illustrative purposes only.

This book is dedicated to my younger self. You are more powerful than you realize. I love you.

Table of Contents

Acknowledgements.. vi
Foreword...ix
Preface...xv
Reflections of Self.. xxi

Part One: Letters of Forgivness

Chapter 1: Learn What Self-Love Is 3
Chapter 2: Know You're Beautiful................... 12
Chapter 3: Remember You're Loveable 27
Chapter 4: You're More Than Enough............ 39
Chapter 5: You've Got This................................ 48
Chapter 6: Say Peace to the Past 58

Part Two: From This Day Forward

Chapter 7: Know What Forgiveness Is............ 72
Chapter 8: Deal with It... 80
Chapter 9: No Validation Needed 87
Chapter 10: Know Yourself................................. 92

Chapter 11: Thank Yourself............................ 100
Epilogue.. 108

Acknowledgements

First and foremost, I thank my Father above for allowing me to birth this baby. Thank You for keeping me through every trial and tribulation just so these words could be spoken. When I cried out in question, You answered me. When I wailed in pain, You comforted me. You have always been there, even when I tried to walk away from my calling, my gifts, and my talents. I turned my back, but You never turned Yours. Thank You.

I have to thank my mama for always believing in me when I didn't believe in myself. Thank you for the lessons that you never knew you were teaching me. Thank you for your many contributions and for loving me when I was unlovable. I believe in you just as much as you believe in me. I love you.

A super special thanks to my other "mama," my big sister, Josie. Thank you for stepping up to the plate when you didn't have to. It wasn't your responsibility. Because of you, I survived. Because of you, I'm here. I often look for ways to show my appreciation, but your heart for giving won't allow you to receive. One day you won't have a choice. I love you more than words can ever say.

I must give a big shout-out to my husband for telling me to speak my truth, no matter what. Your bravery and nonchalant attitude amaze me more than you know. I learn a lot just by watching you. I hear you when you think I don't. You've endured a lot from me because of what I've dealt with. But you never gave up on us. I love you.

My other family, my dad, sisters, brothers, nieces, nephews, cousins, and spiritual family, thank you for the lessons, love, and prayers. I love you all.

To my three heartbeats, C'Nya, Caleb, and Chloe. My beautiful babies. My loves. My lifeline. The three of you have shown me the true meaning of love and forgiveness in more ways I can count. It is my prayer that you continue to shine through your uniqueness. God made you just the way you are and He will use you to continue in the upbuilding of His Kingdom. I love you with every fiber of my being.

To the women who have fought like hell to survive, thank you for never giving up when you had a thousand reasons to. It is my hope that this book speaks volumes. It is my hope that you be encouraged. It is my prayer that you remember who you are and experience self-love like never before. I see you. I love you.

Foreword

Love is being able to find out who you are and accepting everything that God has blessed you with. It is vital to accept all that makes you unique. Embracing yourself and everything about you is the most valuable key to learning how to love yourself. We must realize and understand that we are fearfully and wonderfully made. We are God's handy work and his masterpiece.

Love is being able to clear your mind of every negative feeling and disappointment and appreciating everything about you. Learn to discard every bad thing that has ever been spoken to or about you. Who told you, you were not good enough, your thighs are too big, your hair is too short and nappy, your skin is too dark, or you don't speak correctly? Love is knowing the opposite of every negative word that was said over you.

1 John 4 says, "God is love, and he whose life is full of love, lives in God, and God lives in him." It goes on to say that, "In love, there is not fear, but perfect love drives out all fear, for fear means punishment, and he who fears has not become perfect in love. We love him because he first loved us."

We must love ourselves before we can truly love others. When I was young, things happened to me sexually, and I could not tell anybody. I buried that dark secret until I was an adult. I didn't want to talk to or visit my friends anymore. I asked myself questions such as, "How could this happen to me? Why didn't anybody ask why I went into this shell?" As an adult, I once saw the man that had done those horrible things to me. I saw myself running him over with my car, just seeing him put me back into that dark place. It was as though I was having an out of body experience. This secret started to affect my marriage. There were times that it would be on my mind, and I didn't want to be touched by my husband. This darkness caused a lot of issues between him and me.

Here I was in a marriage, giving him and my family all of me, putting my needs and desires aside to be a wife and mother. I was also juggling duties and responsibilities, such as helping other women. I found myself lost, just living what I thought was the best life. In that, I did not really love myself because I could not be who I was. I did everything others felt that I should, not realizing I had the power to change it. I didn't realize that I had the ability to say what I felt and be who I truly desired to be, so I suppressed all my feelings inside of me. I call this fear.

Years later, my husband betrayed me with numerous affairs. That dark place became more profound. I wanted to know what I'd done wrong. Why wasn't I good enough? I had dreams too. I didn't think that I would ever come out of all this hurt and pain, but God. I heard the voice of God say, "I love you, and I got you." Out of all the hurt and pain, I realized that I must forgive them, but I had to forgive myself most of all. I had to take all that pain before God and ask him to help me forgive those who hurt me. One thing I realized was that forgiveness was my peace.

I prayed and asked God to give me the strength I needed to do what must be done. The more I stayed in that marriage, the more disrespectful he got. I would pray to God, telling him that I didn't want to feel that pain anymore. God took my pain away, and I found myself praying for my husband because he was the one who had low self-esteem. He was the one seeking who and what made him happy.

The most important thing I realized was I was lying to myself; I cheated myself out of true love and life. I knew deep down I had to find out who I was. So, I took a long look in the mirror one morning and said, "Enough is enough! Who are you?" I took a post-it note and wrote, "I AM...." I began to fill it in with, "I am beautiful, powerful." We must know who we are in order to learn to love ourselves.

I have had the opportunity to speak with many different women concerning issues they were having in their lives. The common denominator was self-love. They have all experienced a lot of things from childhood into adulthood. A dark cloud was formed over them because of the terrible things that had happened. Their life issues have caused them to live in unforgiveness. They haven't been honest with themselves about the situations they faced, lying to themselves because it was a family member or a close friend of the family, or someone they trusted.

Tracie is a wife and mom of three lovely children. She is a beautiful, highly intelligent woman who holds degrees from Fort Valley State University. She has experienced some very dark things in her life as well. I can recall the day I received a call to come and go to her house. I was not sure what I was walking into. Once her sister and I arrived, we went upstairs and found her in this drunken state. We saw an empty liquor bottle beside her bed, and she was almost at the point of unconsciousness. My heart went out to her. We then put Tracie in a cold shower; we got in there with her with all our clothes on. I felt and knew that there was something much deeper going on. We asked her questions, but she only stated her kids' names.

I have had the pleasure of watching her grow so much in the church. She became a dance leader, and she would dance with so much passion. I could also see that it was her way to escape, if only for a little while. I have witnessed her come to church as though she did not have a care in the world, but there were times she would come in, and it would be as though she was carrying the world, her own dark secret.

Within this book, you will see that Tracie has come into her truth, and I am so sure it will do the same for you. In these letters, she is sharing her deepest secrets, pain, and unforgiveness. Pressing forward, she is being and doing everything God has ordained her to do. This book will empower you and, for some, maybe even allow you to face the darkness and secrets in your life. It will help you realize that you are not alone. This book is sure to bring about self-awareness; it will empower you to find the true meaning of self-love. In her letters, you will discover the strength to be who you are, and at the same time, awaken the love inside of you.

Tracie has a lot to share. I think it's incredible that she has followed her heart, being obedient to what God has instructed her to do. Some of you will feel like she was right there as you were experiencing a lot of things. It's because she has been there and can understand how you feel. In these letters, you will feel a lot of pain, and awareness will begin to flow from these pages into your heart. Just knowing that God has given her the strength and ability to face her truth and find ways to love herself should give you the strength and power to see that you can too.

May You Be Blessed!
Prophetess Melissa Wood

Preface

Imagine you're hanging out with two of your best homegirls. These are two women that you've known for quite a while. You could have grown up together or met in college; either way, you've been around them long enough to call them your sisters. They are your partners in crime.

One of your friends has struggled in life, and she's a little lost. She's tried her whole life to fit in. What others saw as humility was her awkwardness. She dislikes standing out in the crowd, and she doesn't like to feel like people are noticing her. She hasn't quite discovered how much of an amazing woman she is, worthy of absolute greatness. She has no idea that she doesn't have to accept everything that's placed in front of her. If you were to stand this friend alone and ask her what her interests were or what sets her apart, she wouldn't be able to tell you. She likes whatever is happening at the moment. When your interests change, so does hers. She goes with the flow. Care-free and easygoing. She always criticizes everything about herself. Hiding her true identity, she overexerts herself, trying to change into the person everyone around her wants her to be. She's always negative. She constantly talks down towards herself. Instead of embracing what makes her unique, she finds fault in all she is.

Then, you have your other girl who knows exactly who she is. She's learned to accept everything about herself, and she's proud of who she is and all that she's become. Sister girl genuinely loves who she is. Because of this, she's realized her self-worth and won't settle for anything less than what she feels she deserves. This is the friend that's always positive, treating herself and others well, staying healthy. She's always encouraging you to do the same. She's followed her dreams and is creating her own path. She is the epitome of "living life like it's golden." She is open to the limitless possibilities that are presented to her. She even welcomes all things that challenge her, forcing her to stretch and grow. As far as you know, she rarely complains about the challenges she faces. She knows that she will be an even better version of herself on the other side of those challenges.

We all know someone now or in the past from our inner circle who fits either friend's description. Maybe at one point, that friend was you. What if I told you that both of these friends are one and the same? I was once that friend who shied awkwardly away from the crowd, hoping not to be noticed. But you'd never know because I stood out no matter how hard I tried not to. What was my reason for not wanting to stand out? I never wanted people to get close enough to me to know my insecurities, to know my most intimate thoughts. Then one day, something in me began to slowly change. I was blossoming into that woman who knew just what she wanted and where she was heading.

What changed in me? What brought me from awkwardness to boldness?

Before becoming the person who fell in love with the "woman in the mirror," I was indeed a sad case. Life had become too much for me. I was super unhappy. People on the outside looking in thought I was living the good life. I can't tell you how many times I heard comments like:

"Women would kill to be in your shoes."

"Girl, you got it made. A stay at home wife with a husband who takes care of you."

"That man loves you; he gives you any and everything you ask for."

"You are so beautiful."

"If no one's told you today, you are absolutely gorgeous."

They had no idea that wasn't the life I wanted for myself. They had no idea of the way I viewed myself. I felt like I'd let myself down. Somewhere in my mind, my life's puzzle pieces had been shaken, rearranged, even lost. I felt like I'd screwed myself over. What people saw as me having everything I saw as me not having anything at all.

In a world where every aspect of our lives can be viewed via pictures, videos, and live streaming, it's very easy to get lost in a comparison of what you have versus what someone else has. It can be easy to ignore reality. But whether I had it together or not, I just needed the world to think that I was living my best life. I wanted everyone to believe that I had it all together. I needed them to believe that I was happy and in love with me. But the reality of it was that I was slowly becoming undone. As I said, on the outside looking in, there was nothing wrong with the life I lived. I went to church every Sunday. Every Sunday, I repeated the same declaration before dismissal. Every single Sunday, "I don't live beneath, I live above. I am not the tail; I am the head. I am not down; I'm up. I am not defeated...."

I was married to a good man. My oldest was adjusting reasonably well. I had two beautiful juicy, bouncy babies that laughed at all of my silly faces. But I was unhappy. Something was missing. Maybe I hadn't said my Sunday declaration with enough faith and belief? Perhaps I didn't deserve happiness? Have you ever felt that way? Have you ever reached a point in your life where you genuinely felt like you didn't deserve to be happy? Did you feel like you didn't deserve to smile? Maybe it's just me. But if you have, let me be one of the many to tell you that you deserve to be happy. We all do. There isn't one individual in this world that should walk around every day feeling like happiness isn't for them. I don't care what you've done. I don't care what's been done to you. We all deserve to be happy.

That happiness starts with you. Just as mine did with me, the only way you can obtain happiness is by looking within yourself and choosing happiness daily. Contrary to popular belief, nobody is responsible for your happiness, but you. It isn't anyone else's job to make you smile.

For a long time, I felt it was my husband's job to make me smile. Before that, I thought it was my family's job. After my family, I thought it was my friends' job to make me smile. It was everybody's job, but mine to make me happy. It was their job to bring me joy, to bring me peace. Boy was I wrong. Imagine that rude awakening. When it was all said and done, it all boiled down to one simple thing.

I began to love myself. It turns out, I didn't love me as much as I thought I did. But I figured it out. My goal is to help you as I continue to help myself because self-love is a never-ending journey.

In the upcoming pages, you will find letters I have written to myself, apologizing. They are letters asking forgiveness of myself for all the wrong I've done to myself. Without forgiveness of self, I wouldn't be able to love me wholeheartedly.

Reflections of Self

As I awoke this morning
Peering out at the beauty in the world
I look at myself and say
You're such a beautiful girl

I think to myself
How did I get to this place so new
Knowing there was a time
When just the opposite was true

I used to hear people say
You're sweet and beautiful as can be
I didn't know how they could think that
About someone such as me

I feel good and sometimes bad
Lonely and sometimes sad
There are times when I'm so happy
Then times when I'm quite mad

As I let life happen
I learn about how to love me
Looking at myself, I then began to see
Not the bad, but the good
Others see in me

The more time I spend alone
It's easy to make the choice
I don't need a crowd to talk to

For I love the sound of my own voice

Saying I love myself
Is neither selfish nor conceited
Loving myself means I'm available
And can help if ever I'm needed

I am fearfully and wonderfully made
Created to love me without doubt
This love didn't just happen
It was formed from the inside out

Dollie Carr

Part One

Letters of Forgiveness

Chapter 1

Learn What Self- Love Is

*"Above all else, guard your heart,
for everything you do flows from it."
Proverbs 4:23*

Dear Self,

    Please forgive me for not loving you the way I should have or even at all. There were times when you silently cried out in pain, for healing, peace, and love. I ignored your cries. There were times when I didn't understand who you were or what you wanted. Instead of attempting to figure you out or see what was wrong, I threw you into the arms of another. I was trying to mask your feelings by getting lost in someone else's.

    I am sorry for not taking the time to get to know you in every phase and season of your life. You were forever changing, and I didn't know why or how to keep up. Forgive me for all the negativity I introduced you to. I am sorry for the choices that I made that put you in harm's way. I'm sorry for blaming you for the problems and faults of others. I'm sorry for doubting your greatness and for hindering you from pursuing your dreams and your passion. I'm sorry for allowing you to settle and not pushing you into all of the excellence that I knew you could be. Please forgive me for making you feel like a failure, forcing you into depression and many sleepless nights of crying.

I'm sorry for keeping you occupied with others' problems, never leaving you time to focus on yourself. I'm sorry for giving your power away and allowing those same ones you helped to hurt you. I'm sorry for never listening to you. I apologize for starving you of your much needed time. Your time to heal. Your time to process all that happened over the years. Your time to shine. Forgive me for forcing you to live in fear and defeat.

I'm sorry for not treating you with the utmost respect. I'm sorry for neglecting you and taking you for granted.

The truth of the matter is, I didn't know how to love you. I was afraid of what others would say if I'd chosen to put you first. I didn't want you to be considered selfish. I didn't know how to say "No." I didn't even know that loving you was a necessity or even possible.

Please forgive me.

❤ ❤ ❤

Do you love you? Has anyone ever asked you that question? I've been asked too many times to count. Each time, I would reply, "yes." Then that would be followed up with, "Are you sure?" I'd come right back with an, "I think I love me." I don't know why I was second-guessing whether or not I loved me. It wasn't until therapy that I learned I didn't love myself as much as I thought I did. The therapist told me that I didn't have self-love. Offended, with my head cocked to the side, I challenged her, "What do you mean I don't have self-love?"

"I love me." I was so serious when I said it. I guess it was the fact that I felt like she'd tried me. Like I didn't know what love was. I remember thinking: If I was hungry, I ate. Sometimes. If I felt sick, I went to the doctor. I bathed. I got my hair done every now and again. When I needed necessities, I went and got them. I was taking care of myself. Or so I thought. Apparently, loving yourself meant that you needed to take care of your whole being, the inner woman as well. Self. Who knew? It was then that I learned I didn't think too highly of myself. My self-esteem was low. The way I thought or felt about me was unhealthy. Of course, I didn't learn that until I was left with a blank mind when the therapist told me to say five positive things about myself. Or when she asked what made me, me.

Tell me, standing alone from the crowd, what makes you who you are?

It seems like a relatively simple question, right? Let me put it to you this way. Have you ever been sitting in a job interview and was asked, "Why should we hire you? What makes you different from the rest of the candidates? What are your gifts? What can you offer our company?" Or have you ever needed to sell yourself? I remember during a camp training, we had an activity where we had to market and sell ourselves. When I tell you that was the hardest thing for me to do, it would be an understatement. In either situation, if you aren't prepared, you will be sitting there stuttering your way through an interview or a simple camp activity.

Blank.

That's exactly how I felt when the therapist told me to list five positive traits about myself. Being blank when it comes to you isn't a very comforting feeling. I'm with me every passing second of the day. I should know these things. Had I been asked what makes my mama, my mama, or my dad who he is or even my best friend, I would have been able to provide all kinds of positive traits and attributes back to back.

But when it came to me, it was a completely different story. It's not supposed to be that way because we must know who we are in order to love who we are.

So again, I ask you. Do you love you?

What is self-love?

If we're going to be completely honest, I will tell you that I didn't know those two words' true meaning. What does it mean to love me, and was I capable of genuinely loving me without being selfish? What do you think? Prior to me finding out who I was, I would have said no. Loving myself and caring for me was a downright selfish thing to do. Because if I was so busy focusing on self, how would I be able to focus on others? But the answer is yes; you can love you without being selfish.

As a matter of fact, God wants us to love ourselves. Why would he create us in his image, just for us to turn around and not love ourselves, when God, our creator, is love. However, let's not get self-love confused with narcissism, which is an excessive interest in self or what we call being conceited. Those are all semblances of false love. Self-love isn't the desperate need to feel like you are better than others. Self-love doesn't lack empathy, hurting others. It's quite the opposite. Some may think there's a fragile line between self-love and narcissism. It's all about your attitude and your intentions. Your intentions aren't to hurt anyone in the process of loving yourself. But they are to keep you full so that you can love others in a healthy way.

Let's talk about and define plain old love. We all have different definitions of what love is. I like the words of Paul in 1 Corinthians 13:4-8a. He describes love as being 'patient and kind. He goes on to say that love isn't jealous; it doesn't brag. Love isn't arrogant and rude. Love doesn't seek an advantage. It isn't irritable. Love doesn't keep a record of complaints. Love isn't happy with injustice, but it is happy with the truth.' He continues by saying that 'love puts up with all things, trust in all things, hopes for all things, endures all things. Love never fails.' Paul had a lot to say about what love isn't. Subsequently, it could be easy to effectively deduce what love truly is. Love isn't conditional. Love is strong. It is a force to be reckoned with.

As defined by Oxford, self-love is "regard for one's own well-being and happiness (desirable, not narcissistic or selfish). Self-love means that you take care of your own needs without sacrificing your well-being to please other people. It isn't excessively seeking attention or admiration. It means that you don't settle. You don't settle in life, relationships (familial or romantic), or even with yourself. It means you know your worth. Self-love is motivational. When you choose to love you, I mean genuinely love you, you nurture your total well-being. As a mother nurtures her baby because she knows that her baby would lack in many areas without her, so should you be with yourself. Without your love for self, you would also lack in many areas. Not just physically, but areas such as your personality, your emotions, your mental health. Self-love is caring and having an awareness of self without losing who you are.

Putting those two things together, I'm willing to bet that at some point in your lives, mine included, that we've been impatient with ourselves. We've kept an ongoing checklist about complaints for all the things we've done wrong, forgetting all the things we've done right. We've failed to trust ourselves, our intuition. I've been mean and rude to myself many times. I've walked by the mirror before, stopped, and shook my head. I've called myself stupid. I've cursed myself. Just nasty to the spirit living within me. That isn't loving at all. I can understand why that spirit within me would feel lost, confused, and abandoned. She wasn't loved.

But she deserved to be. You deserve to be. I will admit, it was hard unlearning all the things that I'd told myself. When you're always saying the same thing over and over, it becomes etched into your brain. One of the hardest things for me to do was to learn how to change my mindset. I needed to be intentional with my thoughts and words. Not just me, but you as well. I can't lie and say that change happens overnight. It doesn't. But it happens gradually.

If you've ever felt like you weren't important or undeserving of your own love, let me tell you now, it's time to stop the lies you're telling yourself. Right now. Words are powerful. Proverbs 18:21 says explicitly that "death and life are in the power of the tongue." We have the power to make or break our inner man. We can either build ourselves up or tear ourselves down. For a long time, I was breaking me. Proverbs 23:7 says, "as a man thinketh in his heart, so is he." What you think and say to yourself is what you believe, even if those words aren't true. When I got tired of tearing myself down, when I'd reached my lowest of lows, when I got tired of waddling in my hatred of self, I looked up.

I had nowhere else to go but up. I had nothing else to do but accept that I needed to change. When you can't go any deeper, any lower, you must go up. I'm reminded of a story about a farmer whose goat fell in the well. He wanted to bury the goat because he had no way of getting him out. So the farmer started throwing dirt into the well. With each shovel full going down, the goat shook it off and packed it under his feet until he'd reached the top. The goat refused to give up on himself. Now I am, by no means, comparing you to a goat. However, I am asking you to unpack the self-hatred and stand on it day by day, never giving up on yourself, learning to love yourself genuinely.

❤ ❤ ❤

Self-Love Affirmation: I love me and all that I am.

Chapter 2

Know You're Beautiful

*"You are altogether beautiful, my love;
there is no flaw in you."
Song of Solomon 4:7*

D ear Self,

    Remember when TLC released their song titled Unpretty? You vibed super hard to the lyrics. It was as if they were singing those words just for you. Never mind that the song had a completely different meaning; you related to it all too well. Whatever it was that you didn't like about yourself, you could change it. If you didn't have long hair, you could buy some. If you didn't like your nose, you could get it fixed. You could have loaded your face with all the makeup you could afford. You didn't even wear makeup. But you rocked with it because if there ever was a possibility, options were available. Yet, if you continuously put yourself in positions that made you feel unpretty, whether it was with some boy at the time or some group of girls that made fun of you, you were never going to be happy because you couldn't accept who you were.

After listening to the song just one time, it somehow became your theme song, your mantra. It resonated with every fiber of your being. Little did I know that it was your way of crying out to be accepted. You never wanted to be superficial, but that seemed to be the going trend then because you were always taught that it was what was on the inside that counted. Yet, no one cared enough to look beyond the surface. Because of that, I allowed you to slowly develop into the girl that felt like looks were more important than the heart.

Please forgive me for all the times I thought you were ugly. Allow me to apologize for the times I thought you were too fat. Too skinny. Too dark. I'm sorry for thinking that your forehead was too big, wishing you had smaller feet and bigger breasts. Please forgive me for comparing your looks to others' looks, secretly wishing that you were lighter, had longer loose curled hair, and wishing you were a little bit taller. Forgive me for allowing you to stand in the mirror and pick yourself apart from the crown of your head to the very soles of your feet.

I think back on the time you had the photoshoot, and you uploaded the perfect picture to Facebook, Instagram and any other site that would garner many likes, hearts, oohs, and ahhs. By perfect, I mean, it was flawless. Every lock of hair was in place. Your eyebrows were drawn to a tee. It's funny now because you always talked about people that drew on their eyebrows. Here you were, following the same trend that you hated with a passion. Your eyelashes, although in the way and weighing your eyelids down, were perfectly lined. Your makeup was heavily contoured to perfection, clogging all of your pores. Your lips were popping. Crooked smile and all, and the sun hit your skin just right, making you glow like an African Goddess.

You smiled and soaked it all in. It made you feel good, truly beautiful. You basked in it all. Nothing else on that day mattered. If someone had told you that you weren't all that, their thoughts wouldn't have counted in that moment.

Then you washed your face.

The sink was full of brown gunk, with splashes of black here. Speckles of gold there. A little bit of red. The long, beautiful eyelashes had been pulled off and were lying beside the sink. There was a disgusting ring of what previously was.

You walked around for four hours, feeling like you owned the room and everything outside of it. Reflecting the words of Raheem the Dream, in your mind, you were "the most beautiful girl in the world."

It all went down the drain, literally.

As you looked in the mirror, there were no more glittery shimmers in your eyes' corners. There was no more winged tipped eyeliner. No more red lips. No more flawless skin.

Just plain old you, a brown-skinned girl with big eyes, a big forehead, thin lips, unruly eyebrows, keloid ears, and dry skin.

You looked at yourself with disgust and walked away. Little did you know that your baby boy had been watching you. Remember what he asked and said? "Mommy, why did you have on all that makeup?" You told him that you had a photoshoot and asked if he liked it. With absolutely no filter nor pausing, he responds with, "No, it's ugly. You look pretty without it." Then he walked away. One thing you can't deny is the way it made you feel because we all know kids will boldly speak their minds with nothing but authenticity.

The truth of the matter is that I allowed other people's insecurities and their views of you to sway your thoughts of yourself. I used to think that you were super pretty, but people always talked about how dark you were, and the jokes they made broke you down little by little each day. When others told you that you were conceited for walking around with your head held high, you began to lower it, even though you knew you didn't think on such an arrogant level. You didn't want others to say it, so you dialed it back a bit. Only to get up one day, completely forgetting about who you were. I'm sorry for allowing you to ignore your natural beauty and for allowing others to tarnish your view of self.

Please forgive me.

❤ ❤ ❤

Except for those who know me, I'm sure people see my pictures and think, "now there's a woman who looks like she's in love with herself. She gets up, looks in the mirror, and smiles at the face looking back at her because she knows that she's gorgeous."

I know this to be true because I've heard it before after posting a selfie with the caption "I woke up like this" at the break of dawn when the brightness hit my face just right through the blinds. Making my brown eyes glisten and sparkle as it does the ocean after an unsettling storm.

I hate to be the bearer of bad news to those who don't truly know me. Even to those who think they know me. Underneath this smile, my self-esteem was in shambles. I didn't like how my mouth curved slightly more to the right when I smiled, exposing a baby tooth that never fell out. Or how my eyes wrinkled in the corners. Or how the tip of my nose does this weird thing, pointing downward. Heaven forbid if there wasn't enough lighting to cast a glow on my skin. Then I felt like an ashy blur.

Despite all the comments I got on the one picture I decided to share with the world, after taking fifty selfies and searching for THE PERFECT one to showcase what's supposed to be how pretty I felt about myself that day, I never truly felt it. Whew, there I said it. I secretly hated who I was because I didn't think I was pretty enough. I didn't look like so and so. You know, that pretty dark-skinned model or actress I secretly admired. Wishing and hoping that one day I will have the perfect confidence that they have. To be able to post the one picture, criticizing everything about me, while still being able to maintain the most flawless look ever. You know how they do. They post this picture, complaining about the simplest thing, only to have a million and one fans comment on their perfection.

The perfect smile.

The perfect eyes.

The perfect teeth.

The perfect body.

Just pure perfection.

I have told myself so many lies. I believed the many lies pasted to the front of the most popular magazines that captured just a few seconds of exquisiteness for only a moment. Forgetting that these beautiful masterpieces are human just like me. Covered in makeup just as I was on the day I posted that stunning photo, feeling like a million bucks. The truth is, I'm not too fond of makeup. Actually, I hate makeup. But I wanted to keep up with the frivolous thoughts of the world.

While inside, I was falling apart.

How often do you criticize your body without even realizing that's what you're doing? Sure we've all tried on a pair of pants that no longer fit, and we immediately called ourselves fat. But let's be honest, it's because we've been holding onto those jeans for the last ten plus years. Do you know how much our bodies change in just a couple of years? Then again, it could have only been an off day. Our bodies are always fluctuating. One day our weight hits just right; the next, it somehow shifts to places we didn't know we had. Don't get me started on the bodies that have carried other little humans. We love our children, but honey, they will do a number on our bodies.

It's no secret that we criticize our bodies, especially today in an age where everything is plastered all over the internet, and body shaming has become a sickening normal. Before the internet, we were only competing with television ads and magazine articles. Now every time you open your phone, you have access to the lives of everyone portraying false perfections and fake securities. Don't allow those five-hundred likes to fool you. Most women, including myself, criticize their bodies at least five to six times a day. But it's not deliberate.

Take, for instance, when someone compliments your hair. What's the first thing we might say? "Girl, it's nappy." Or they compliment your outfit. "I need to tone up; I need to lose ten pounds. I need to do this or that." They said absolutely nothing about your weight. Instead of saying "thank you," we run down a list of things that we 'need' to do in hopes of them making us appear more appealing. When in reality, we are beautiful just the way we are. Otherwise, we wouldn't have gotten that compliment. Sidebar, I was talking to myself right there. I have a terrible habit of thwarting compliments because sometimes I feel like I don't deserve them. Isn't it something that we, as women, will compliment each other every day, but won't say those same words to ourselves?

Social media has ruined our way of thinking. Music videos, makeup companies, reality shows, and the likes have made it so hard to accept ourselves as we were created. We've allowed society to place such high value on fabricated beauty.

When I say fabricated beauty, I'm talking about forcing us to believe that we need to have long silky hair, hazel green eyes, big butts, and huge breasts to be gorgeous. So we go out and spend thousands of dollars on wigs, makeup, silicone, and saline to please people that won't ever see us in real life. We've seen the celebrities that spend thousands of dollars on becoming so unrecognizable. I can't imagine those people loving themselves, putting their bodies through so much harm.

Don't get me wrong; there's absolutely nothing wrong with any of these things if, at the end of the day, when the wig and makeup come off, you still feel beautiful inside. If you're doing those things as a part of YOUR self-love and self-care routine, not for the approval of outside influences, then you're good. Otherwise, you're going to be forever talking negatively to yourself every time you fail to meet others' standards. Or the standards that you've set based on the looks of other people. This way of being will cause a problem because each time you miss the mark, you will end up feeling down and out, depressed. I was there, and I had to make some heartfelt changes.

One thing I had to do was stop comparing myself to others. Comparing caused me to have unrealistic expectations, such as thinking that I would be down twenty-five pounds in one week after drinking some detox tea. That wasn't happening. Those advertisements we see are all lies, using photoshop and women that can stand to eat a sandwich or two.

If you want to lose weight, go for it. Walk thirty minutes a day. But do it because you want to, not because some commercial says you have to be a size zero to go to the beach. If you want to gain weight, go for that too. If you want to change anything about yourself, by all means, go for it. But as I stated before, do it for you. Not because you saw a picture of someone you went to school with, and they look like they haven't gained an ounce since graduating high school. As I stated, social media will have us feeling like failures if we allow it.

That is why it is imperative to limit the amount of time you spend on your favorite websites. Believe it or not, there is a link between how we feel about ourselves and the amount of time we spend perusing the world wide web. We end up scrutinizing our bodies and others' bodies because we aren't as confident as some think we may be. Why do you think there's so much body shaming going on? People are comparing when they shouldn't be. We are truly living in a filtered lens world.

Change your circle. Whew, that's a tough one. Your inner circle, those you spend a significant amount of time with, has a significant influence on your life. These are the people who pretty much determine how you dress, where you eat, and most definitely how you view yourself. So who are you hanging with? Okay, maybe not change your whole circle because I understand those people have been your ride or die forever. A better suggestion would be to find others who can add more flavor to the group or seek other friends who appeal to the person you are trying to become.

In the meantime, there are a few things that can help you and your current circle shift for the better. For starters, you can opt-out of having that pity fest every time you're with your people that are always complaining or tearing themselves down. You know the pity fest of complaints I'm referring to. You can sense when it's coming on. It's usually around that time you're all getting ready to go out, and you see a bunch of outfits lying around the floor, and then you hear that deep gut groan coming up. Or when either one of you is having a displeasing day.

Stop it before it even gets started. Change the subject. Don't even allow the negative talk to begin. As women, it is a must that we learn how to be more comfortable with uplifting each other, complimenting one another. Strangers do it all the time. There's absolutely nothing wrong with telling your best friend how gorgeous and fine she is. When she gets in a funk about her appearance based on what she saw online, remind her of her beauty.

Your inner circle should include people who leave you feeling supported, uplifted, and inspired, not questioning everything about yourself. Surround yourself with a group of friends who randomly screams out, "Yaaaaaas chic" when you enter the room. Believe me when I tell you, it makes a world of difference.

Another thing, lower your tone when you talk to you. Have you ever heard someone say that to another person? Or "don't talk to me like that." The same thing goes for you. Brene Brown once said, "Talk to yourself like you would someone you love." We talk to people differently when we really care about and love them. This applies to yourself. Change the way you talk to you. It's so easy to speak negatively to ourselves. We must make a conscious effort to speak positivity into our own lives.

I remember, as a teacher, I would hear the students that I worked with speak words of "I can't, or I'm not." Each time I heard them say they couldn't do something or they weren't good enough; I would stop them right there and tell them to say two positive things about themselves. It was hard for them at first, but eventually, they changed how they spoke about who they were because they knew that Mrs. Johnson was going to make them say something positive.

This same rule applies to me, as well as you. I'll be honest; there are days when I don't feel like I can get anything right, from my hair to my shoes. But then there are some days I stand in the mirror, and I talk to myself like I'm a brick house! Just between you and me, I'll turn around and jiggle my booty like I got dollars being thrown at me. Don't judge me. Do I feel like this every day? Absolutely not, but I have to put in the effort until I do.

Whatever you don't like about yourself, you can work to change it, or you can think about all the things you love about yourself. However, on those days where I feel like I can't get anything right or I'm not feeling my best, I have to make my most extraordinary attempt to speak positive affirmations. Let yourself know that it's okay to make mistakes. I must thank my church in assisting with this because they will be quick to put us on a fast from speaking negatively. I am thinking, so wait, "you want me to give up cookies and negative words?!? Yeah. No, I can only do one at a time."

In all seriousness, it's not something that will happen overnight. It's most certainly not something that you do one time and think you have mastered it. Believe me; baby steps are required and welcomed. Changing how you talk to yourself is an ongoing process. Allow me to let you in on another secret; it helps to write them down. Go back to what I would do with my students. Write those negative thoughts down, but cancel out every negative phrase with a positive comment. It doesn't matter if you put those words in a notepad, on an index card, or a sticky note, as long as you release the negative talk.

♥ ♥ ♥

Self-Love Affirmation: I am beautiful. I am a human work in progress.

Chapter 3

Remember You're Loveable

"Love must be sincere..."
Romans 12:9

Dear Self,

    Please forgive me for forcing you to stay in toxic relationships that clearly weren't good for you, causing you way too much emotional pain. Nobody deserves to endure the kind of heartache I watched you go through. I'm sorry for making you stay with guys who repeatedly accused you of doing wrong, only to find out that they were projecting their insecurities onto you. I apologize for standing by and watching you allow them to make a fool of you over and over again with the phone calls from multiple females and the drive-bys, proving to you time and time again that they were never going to change for you. No woman should have to wonder if she's the only one in a man's life. Nor should she always question her self-worth because of other beings' hang-ups.

Forgive me for making you feel like you could change any of them. You all but depleted yourself doing something that wasn't your job to do, and in your thinking of trying to change someone, you lost sight of who you were. In all of that, you began to realize that none of the things you used to do made you happy. You began to think that you were seriously flawed. You wanted to change them so badly that you ended up changing and losing sight of yourself, losing who you were. You didn't deserve any of that because nobody will change unless it's something they want to do. I allowed you to blame yourself for their shortcomings instead of helping you realize that it wasn't you at all. I'm also sorry for allowing you to settle time after time.

I'll never forget that time you curled up in your mama's chair in the corner of the living room and cried your eyes out in the dark for hours on end. You were full of so much confusion and hurt. You kept asking yourself what was wrong with you; why you weren't good enough. I wanted to help you, but I didn't know what to say. So instead of telling you that he wasn't worth it, I just stood by and watched you go back to him over and over again, only to end up disappointed every single time.

I know that he told you he loved you, but in all honesty, he had no idea what real love was. The only thing he loved was the fact that you were naive enough to believe that he was your good thing. He loved the fact that he could use and abuse you, and you weren't going to leave. He loved that he could talk down to you, walk all over you, making himself feel superior. He loved how you'd bend over backward for him and not ask for anything in return. He never really loved you, only what you did for him.

Please forgive me for not speaking up every time I noticed the red flags that something wasn't right. I get it; the guy had the most amazing smile, and he told you things you wanted to hear. In those moments, his lies were everything. I know that in those moments, you had the tiniest bit of hope. So that's what I allowed you to hang on to for so long. Hoping they'd change. Hoping they'd notice the small things you did. Hoping they'd hear your silent cries.

I'm sorry for making you feel like any attention was good attention, as long as someone noticed you. I know you thought that maybe one day he'd wake up and realize how much he was hurting you. You even believed him when he said that he would. Only to find yourself back at square one, questioning everything about who you were.

Please allow me to apologize for the insecurity you felt every time he smiled when his phone rang, but he sent it to voicemail.

Most of all, I apologize for allowing you to enter into everything that looked and felt like a relationship, never giving you the time to heal, detox, and unpack the baggage from the previous one. Instead, I allowed you to pile all the hurt on, burdening your heart with too much garbage. You no longer knew what it was about you that made you who you were. You'd become someone that not even your family recognized. You'd forgotten what made you happy. You no longer remembered your own strength. You'd forgotten who you were. Your heart was too big. Even then, you cared more about hurting him than you did about your own pain in staying.

The truth of the matter is, I was afraid of you being alone. Rather than being alone, I allowed you to settle for a mediocre guy who treated you like you were a footstool. Even though I knew deep down that these relationships wouldn't be beneficial to you, I mean some of these guys treated their cars better than they treated you. I wanted you to stay because I was afraid you'd feel like you failed at yet, another relationship. I didn't want you to bear that kind of shame, no matter how unhappy you were and how bad you were hurting. I felt like you needed them.

You needed them to make you feel like you were somebody. Make you feel special. After all, all the women wanted them, but they'd chosen you. Every time they said or did something to hurt you, they'd apologize and treat you to things you always wanted to do. They even brought you flowers. That counts for something, right? It was as if you'd become desperate and needy.

But I now realize how much damage that caused your psyche and how low it made your self-esteem. I see now how it added more to your feelings of inadequacy and your thoughts of not being good enough. You walked away each time with more and more doubt of your worth as a woman. I see now that every time someone new came along, you lost more and more of yourself. Until one day, you looked up and had no idea who you were. I understand the harm and destruction this caused to your emotional and mental state.

Please forgive me.

♥ ♥ ♥

"How could I have been so stupid?"

"Who am I?"

"I don't know this person anymore."

"How could I allow this to happen to me?"

"What's wrong with me?"

There's no doubt in my mind that you have secretly asked yourself some form of those questions at some point in your life. If you're anything like me, you may have found yourself in the mirror, on the floor, or in your car, with tears in your eyes and snot running out of your nose, asking loudly, "why doesn't he love me?" I've even had my 'sitting outside his door moments, waiting." But that's another story for another day. I have been delivered from all of my crazy thinking ways. But that just further proves the effects that toxic relationships can have on a person.

Anytime we come out of any toxic or dysfunctional relationship, we need to do a mental and emotional detox. Detox? Yes, the same way it's necessary to do a physical detox, we must also cleanse our minds of unhealthy thoughts and emotions that we have endured. We have to reshift and declutter. I don't know about you, but I have to reshift and declutter my mind on a regular basis, and this has nothing to do with being in a toxic relationship. Imagine the mental junk you have after a dysfunctional relationship. We're human, and because our thoughts are sometimes the very thing that's holding us back, we have to check our thoughts in all things continually.

Proverbs 23:7 reads, "as someone thinks within himself, so he is." What you think within yourself, what you feel to be true about yourself, will be if you continue to believe it to be so. That is why it's imperative that we detox our minds. We may have come out of a relationship, thinking that we aren't worthy because that's what we were told or felt. If we left a relationship feeling like everything we did was wrong, our minds have embedded within us that something is wrong. When, in fact, nothing was wrong with us. The person didn't know how to receive what we had to give. Believe you me, it had nothing to do with you, but everything to do with them. I know we've all heard that tired saying, "it's not you; it's me." Believe them when they tell you, because queen, it's not always you.

Mentally detoxing after a relationship that wasn't good for your spirit and soul takes time. It starts with forgiveness. It would help if you forgave yourself first. The most important relationship you have in this world, outside of God, is the one you have with yourself. You're with you, twenty-four seven, and there is no escaping that. No matter how hard you try. I say that you have to forgive yourself, not because you knew better, but because many times when we enter into a relationship, it isn't toxic right off the bat.

In the beginning, it's all good. The changes can be so subtle that you don't realize the damage that's being done over time. There's nothing wrong with that; we've all been there some time or another. So first and foremost, don't punish yourself for being human; forgive yourself.

Next, we have to stop overthinking and overdoing. Overthinking in any relationship almost always comes from past hurts. When we've been in a toxic relationship for so long, we began to second guess everything we do. Not only that, we question the quality of the relationship based on past situations. Even years after the relationship has ended. This is why detoxing is important. We were slowly conditioned into believing negative things about ourselves. When so much time and effort is being put into someone who doesn't appreciate and deserve what you have to offer, you begin to wonder if something is wrong with you. Nothing's wrong; you have to stop looking at yourself through the eyes of those who meant you no good.

In order to stop overthinking and overdoing, remember who you are. Start your day empowered. Pray. One thing for certain, two things for sure, "you are more than a conqueror." You are more than what someone made you feel. You are strong. You are powerful. You are an overcomer.

When in a toxic relationship, sometimes we have a tendency to become obsessive. Whether it's trying to be the perfect mate for someone who doesn't deserve us or trying to fix ourselves. Take that energy, and focus on something more positive. Focus on you.

One thing I learned about myself after a break-up is that I could draw. I had no idea. I mean, I'm no Picasso, but it's good enough to display in my own home. I remember sitting on the floor, and I had this poster board and a pencil. I just started drawing. Then I focused my attention on a picture that was in my room.

About two hours later, I had a picture of Pooh and Piglet that'd been drawn, colored, and placed on my wall. I'd drawn my obsessive thoughts away. Find something creative and productive. I know it may take a while but think back on some of your favorite activities you enjoyed doing before that relationship changed you. It could be something that you placed on the backburner. Go back to it. If you like to write, write. Writing is the perfect way to get those thoughts out. Suppose you're good with your hands, you can craft and build. Like to cook or bake, go for it. Let me insert a disclaimer here. Please be very careful with cooking and baking. These activities have been known to cause unwanted weight gain. I don't need you looking for me, saying, "Tracie said, cook..." Because the only thing I'm going to do is sit down beside you and eat. Saying "now look at us, we are both fat and happy!" All I'm saying is, cook, and bake in moderation. Who knows, maybe that creative productivity can turn into something far greater than you expected, like a business.

Talk to someone. I had a bad habit of isolating myself from others. Isolation left me with my own negative thoughts. Being left with negative thoughts is a big no-no because the whole object is self-love, healing, and forgiving yourself. So if you're isolating yourself with no positive influences or advice, it can cause even more damage.

The catch with this one though is to talk to someone that you know without a shadow of a doubt you can trust and someone who will truly uplift you. You need an individual who will speak life and love into you. You want someone who can pray for you and someone who won't share your intimate conversations with anyone else. For me, it was a good friend who understood just what I was dealing with because she'd experienced similar things. For you, it could be a family member, someone at church, or a support group of women who have had like experiences. No matter who it is, you want that person to be positive with the ability to help you uplift yourself.

My all-time personal favorite way to detox, is music. There are moments where I will sing and dance my way into peace, love, and happiness. I am a firm believer that music is therapeutic. Music is healing. Music creates an energy that connects deeply within our souls. It has the power to change how we think, feel, and process. There's a reason why our mothers and grandmothers used to put on music while cleaning on Saturday mornings. They could clean a whole house in what seemed like minutes because of music. It gets you going. I don't think I can stress enough how important music is. It holds a timeline.

We can almost, always pinpoint a moment in time based on a song. What better way to make you feel good and fall in love with you than by singing and dancing? Purposefully choose an upbeat song, something that has meaning. Try to refrain from choosing something that is sure to bring you down or something with negative ties related to it. Listen to the song and embrace the way it makes you feel. My all-time favorites are Cyndi Lauper's, *Girls Just Want to Have Fun* and Whitney Houston's, *I Wanna Dance with Somebody*. Put on a whole concert if you have to. But let go, it's just you. Enjoy yourself in that moment.

Let me not leave you without saying this: Because I don't know where you are in life and your relationship status, allow me to give you helpful advice. If you are in a physically or mentally abusive relationship or if this relationship is causing you to question if life is worth living, please seek immediate help.

❤ ❤ ❤

Self-Love Affirmation: I am lovable and I am loved. I love myself.

Chapter 4

You're More Than Enough

"Arise my darling, my beautiful one."
Song of Solomon 2:10

Dear Self,

    Please forgive me for thinking you weren't good enough. I know there have been plenty of times you wanted to try something new or do something different, but I talked you out of it. I did all I could to make sure you felt like new endeavors were impossible, and that you would fail. I made sure to cloud your mind with all of the things that could possibly go wrong. Even when you talked up the courage to go for it, I always found an excuse to hinder you from moving forward.

    Like when you wanted to try out for basketball, and I told you that there was no way possible, you'd be able to shoot a jump shot because you were too short. I knew you were never going to make the team. Where, in all the history of basketball, have you ever seen a short-stature person play? Instead of allowing you to find someone to practice with before tryouts and allowing them to teach you about the different positions you would have probably been good at, I just said, "No, you won't be good enough." When in reality, with enough practice, you probably could have been one hell of a point guard because of your attitude and desire to see everyone win.

Or that time you wanted to go into the Air Force, but I told you no because your hearing wasn't up to par. You were never going to be good enough for that. I just knew you'd fail because you need A1 hearing to be in the military. How were you going to defend your country when you could hardly hear? It doesn't matter that you exceeded in everything during the physical, the doctor told you to get a hearing test done, and everything would have been handled from that point on. Instead of allowing you to follow your path and hone in on your excellent leadership skills, I told you, "No, you won't be good enough." When in reality, you would have made one badass officer because of your intelligence and integrity. Besides, who doesn't love a woman in uniform? I know that I never told you, but sis your scores on the ASVAB were incredible!

The truth of the matter is, I was afraid for you. I didn't want you to be talked about and ridiculed even though the majority of the girls who were playing and trying out were the same height as you. But I was trying to protect you. Or at least I thought I was. I now realize that I stifled your growth. I hindered any possibilities of what could have been in the event that you'd made a great player, moving on to becoming an even greater leader, helping other females who were thinking they were too short. Or in the event, you'd made an excellent officer, uplifting others around you, producing more leaders with integrity, honesty, and creativity.

That draining mentality of not being good enough stuck with you for a very long time. I made you question and second guess every new thing you wanted to try. I know you missed out on many opportunities, but I won't stop you from this day forward.

Please forgive me.

♥ ♥ ♥

It sucks, doesn't it? Feeling like you're not good enough is draining. It may not feel that way for you, but it most certainly does for me. I can't count the number of times I've talked myself out of what could have possibly been the best experience of my life because I felt like I didn't have what it took to succeed. When in reality, I did. All I needed was a little extra push from inside.

When we talk ourselves out of experiences, we're often left sitting and singing what my mama calls the "shoulda, coulda, woulda." It's honestly not a good feeling or place to be in. I realize that this day in age, it's easy to sink into that feeling of inadequacy. We live in a digital age where people regularly post their filtered lives on social media for the world to see, causing us to get stuck comparing ourselves. But remember this, if you don't remember anything else, the people we are watching and comparing our lives to are probably comparing their lives to someone else. None of us have it all together.

When did that feeling of not being good enough even begin? Where did it come from? Perhaps it started somewhere in your childhood when you brought home B's and C's, and your sibling came home with A's. You saw how highly those A's were praised and maybe how they even garnered ten dollars apiece. Your B's only brought in five dollars apiece, of course, nothing for the C's. So you buckled down and gave it your all every single quarter, but no matter how hard you tried, your best wasn't good enough. Your best didn't receive the recognition. So you stopped giving it your all, you quit trying, leaving you with the lasting effects of a vicious cycle that would become hard to break.

It doesn't matter when it began or how long ago it was, unless it's nipped at the beginning, feelings of inadequacy will continue to linger and disrupt your life. You will always be left feeling like you're not good enough. These feelings will rob you of so many possibilities to shine and show others around you what a great individual you are. If you aren't careful, they will cause you to overexert yourself, pushing yourself further into a place you shouldn't be in mentally and emotionally. We must recognize that the feeling of not being good enough is one from within. Although we may be surrounded by people who make us feel like we aren't good enough, we have the power and the ability to reject the negativity.

The feeling of not being good enough leads to overcompensation, then we begin to undervalue ourselves. My mama always told me that I was a perfectionist. Everything had to be perfect. I used to think that it was a compliment because it meant that I was very thorough and detailed at everything I did. However, I later learned that it was a character flaw of mine. I was pushing myself beyond normal stress levels, burning myself out because I was trying to make up for the feeling of not being noticed. I was trying to stand out. I would go at something for hours on end until it met my satisfaction, no matter what others said. What I thought was me going above and beyond, trying to achieve greatness, I was overcompensating.

I remember years ago when I was beyond stressed out with school and a relationship that I was in; I had a friend teach me how to rid my mind of negativity. He said, "Tracie, lie on your back, breathe in and out slowly. As you breathe in, imagine that it's a white cloud. It was supposed to be a cloud of peace and joy. When you exhale, imagine it being green. The green is the negative thoughts, the garbage that you've ingested, and internalized. The garbage that you've believed to be true, but it wasn't." With each breath in, I saw all the things I was good at, and with each breath out, I exhaled every feeling and thought of not being good enough.

Now, don't get me wrong; it sounded like a dumb thing to do at the time because I had to actively force myself to focus on my breathing. I had to forcefully focus on being positive and discard all the negativity. Surprisingly, after about fifteen minutes of purposeful breathing, I felt like I could do anything.

In fact, we can do anything. It may not come as easy to us as it would with others, but we can do anything. One of my favorite movies of all time is Dirty Dancing. Francis, lovingly known as Baby, was given the task of taking over for Penny as Johnny's dance partner. She didn't feel like she had what it took because I mean, Penny was a fantastic dancer. But during the movie, we would see Baby practicing and giving it her all. She eventually became just as great as Penny, if not better, killing that last dance scene that had everyone up on their feet. Imagine the regret she would have had, had she stuck with her feelings of not being "good enough."

To move past the doubt and negativity, becoming the best at whatever we want, we must recondition our way of thinking. Easier said than done, I know. But I promise you, the small steps you take will be worth your journey to learning how to love yourself.

- ♥ Think about what it is that you're overcompensating for. Think about how it's affecting your mental state. Then exhale your negative thoughts out. Just as my friend had me breathing in and out, you too can do it. I promise you, as silly as it sounds, it works. Negative thoughts are inevitable. We're human, it happens. But instead of dwelling on them, turn them green and let them dissipate. Then inhale.

- ♥ Celebrate your small steps on the way. Everything won't always come naturally.

Sometimes you have to take smaller steps in order to get to greatness. And sometimes on your way to greatness, you may end up taking three steps forward and five steps backward. But with each step you take forward, celebrate. With each step you take backward, learn. Believe it or not, you can celebrate your failures because you wouldn't be moving without them. Be mindful of your successes, no matter how small they are. Remember, progress is more remarkable than perfection.

♥ Limit your time on social media. Now, this is a hard one. I can say this because I live on Facebook and Instagram. But I can't tell you how good I felt the many times I made the conscious effort to pull away and shut it all down. In doing this, I limited the lies I told myself about how so and so's life was much better than mine. I mean, everybody's life is perfect on social media. Yours is too because we filter it all.

♥ Pray. Meditate. Ground yourself. Whatever it is that you do, please do it. Prayer and meditation are definite ways to change your mind and deter you from the negative feelings and thoughts of not being good enough. Philippians 4:13 reads, "For I can do everything through

Christ, who gives me strength." That verse alone makes you GOOD ENOUGH!

♥ Remember that you have already achieved a great deal in life; you've overcome a lot. You may not be living your best life, but I guarantee that someone looking at you feels different. Remember all of the things that you have accomplished. Remember how you felt when you just knew you were good enough. Choose to focus on that, while you continue to put your best foot forward.

❤ ❤ ❤

Self-Love Affirmation: I am more than enough.

Chapter 5

You've Got This

"She is vigilant over the activities of her household; she doesn't eat the food of laziness."
Proverb 31:27

Dear Self,

Please forgive me for putting you on the backburner after marriage and more children. Although you went about it as some would consider "backward," it was the first, most promising relationship you'd had. It was a relationship full of stability, potential, and limitless possibilities. You already knew how things were probably going to turn out. Besides, you'd prepared for this lifestyle your whole life. As with most other little girls, you'd practiced this since you were young, playing the imaginary game House with your baby dolls. Your man was perfect. Your children were the best children you'd ever seen. You had your fulfilling dream job and came home to smiling faces every day. Cooked dinner and ate at a table filled with love and laughter every night. You went on vacation twice a year, sometimes three, with your best girlfriends. You'd picnic in the park on Saturdays and go to church on Sundays. You'd hardly ever argue, and when you did, you'd make up because you were both two loving people and wanted to maintain a peaceful environment for the family. You'd had millions of conversations and scenarios filed away to fall back on for any and every event that could possibly come up in your marriage.

In the beginning, it was what some considered their dream set-up. It was the type of family and relationship you only saw on television. He worked, you stayed home, cooked, cleaned, and took care of the babies. You made sure to stay on top of all the bills so that he'd be able to focus on the more pressing things. You didn't want him to worry about anything that was going on inside the house since he had to handle what was going on at work. Everything was working. You had it managed.

Until you didn't.

He'd decided to go active duty. Not only that, but he felt that you needed to work harder than you already were at finding a job because you guys were struggling, and he needed help. Then he told you that you weren't the girl he thought he'd married. He was expecting somebody determined and hardworking. He was expecting a go-getter. After all, you'd gone to college and graduated with two degrees. Never mind that you were going on interviews belly out because you were pregnant. Never mind that you'd had two babies back to back, literally in the same year. Never mind the fact that all of these things were way down on your list of "Life Goals." Your plans and how you wanted your life to go had been "flipped and turned upside down." Mama always said that if you wanted to hear God laugh, tell him your plans. I know God is forever laughing at me.

Regardless of all the preparation you'd made for your perfect marriage, no amount of playing House could have prepared you for the postpartum depression and the downhill spiraling to come. You threw yourself into overdrive, trying to be the person he thought he'd married. Trying to be the catch he thought he had. Your mind was always on the go, looking for ways to make money and bring in some kind of income, adding more and more to the feeling of already not being good enough. No matter how many times he assured you that you were the woman he wanted to marry, deep down, you always felt like you really weren't the one, and it was the babies that kept you two together. But you pushed forth nonetheless because you are a fighter, and giving up has never been in your DNA. You went to counseling, crying your eyes out in confusion and turmoil, seeking some semblance of relief. Only to leave each session feeling like it didn't matter how much effort you put into your marriage, everything was somehow your fault. In all of that, trying to be a better wife and a great mother, you lost yourself even more. You forgot what made you, you.

The truth is, nothing could have prepared you for marriage and all the things that it brings. Of course, premarital counseling is an option that you can choose to partake in, but that preparation is more so for conflict resolution and discussing communication strategies. There aren't enough teachings and role modeling or playing in the world to tell you how to love yourself, your man, and your kids simultaneously.

Sometimes we go into marriage, winging it on hope and a prayer. There is no cookie-cutter manual because every individual in every relationship is different. Without knowing how to love yourself and not be looked at as selfish, you're pretty much stuck until you figure it out. What you may not know is that you can love yourself in a marriage and not be selfish. You can take some time for yourself without feeling guilty for having to do so. There is absolutely nothing wrong with having some "you" time. It doesn't mean that you despise the life that you've created. It means you're human, and you need to recoup. Self-care is vital in any relationship to your well-being and peace of mind.

Please forgive me for allowing you to feel like you were a bad person because there were some moments in your life where you questioned whether you could succeed in your marriage while holding on to you. You most certainly can, and just in case I forget, you're ROCKING this thing!

♥ ♥ ♥

As women, we often forget that we're individuals who have needs of our own outside of the family. We get so wrapped up in being the ideal wife and mother, and we forget to be who we are. We lose track of ourselves and our uniqueness. Sometimes we let go of our individuality because anything else would be considered self-centered. Heaven forbid if we try to hold on to some sense of self, decide to take a weekend with friends for some much-needed self-recovery, the guilt is insanely overwhelming. I did that once. Needless to say, I hardly enjoyed my time at the beach because I was so concerned about what was going on at home and worried about whether or not I was going to go back to a house hanging on threads. Or whether or not I was going to catch flack about my getaway somewhere down the line.

When we are torn between making sure we take care of our needs, time alone, and our family's needs, we feel stretched. Feelings of guilt when we finally decide to step away for a few hours or even a weekend take away from the intended purpose of recouping. In the long run, feelings of guilt could cause bitterness towards self and the relationship. This guilt can lead to even more problems that could have been avoided.

We have to remember that even in marriage, we are continually evolving. Therefore, we have to rediscover ourselves over and over again. Our needs, wants, and desires change. We have to revamp, so to speak. Know that it's okay to have to go back to the drawing board. My mama tells me often that life has a funny way of coming at you, and sometimes you have to change your plans. Change is inevitable. Granted, it took me a little longer than most to understand what this meant for my family and me. But when I figured it out, my goodness, there was no stopping me. I was, indeed, the person he'd married. I was still determined. I was still a go-getter. Just not in the way he thought I should be. I learned that there was no need for me to feel bad for his perception of me because his life experiences determined how he saw me. It did not dictate who I was in my core.

As a woman, a wife, a mother, we have to remember that everyone perceives things differently. Just because someone sees you one way doesn't mean that you are the way that they see you. You know who you were and who you could be. Also, you must admit that you may not be the person someone expects you to be. However, this begins with acceptance. You must acknowledge and accept everything about you. Nobody has the right to make you feel inadequate about who you truly are. Not even you, and if you're unhappy with anything you consider flaws, change them. If there are some things you can't change, then unapologetically accept them.

If you've been in a relationship for quite some time, get to know the new you. You're not the same person you were six or seven years ago. You have been through changes, some subtle, some not so much. Your new and more evolved inner being is dying for your attention, and I promise you do have all it takes to love her, your spouse, and your children. In all of that, just remember to be the best you that you can be; while keeping in mind that self-care isn't just a mere passing desire. It's essential because self-care is giving yourself all of you when you need you most.

There are some things to consider when in a relationship or even when you're not, with or without children. As I stated, there is no cookie-cutter manual for any relationship; however, we all need some form of time for self when we are devoting our time to others. Make sure to:

♥ Discuss ahead of time with your mate the need for self-care. Because we all have our own definitions of what self-love and self-care is, talk about what that may look like. Assure your partner that it doesn't take away from your love for them. Let them know that in renewing yourself, you can stay refreshed in the relationship. Accept when your partner needs their time and use that break to cater to your needs.

♥ Don't wait until the last minute when you're at the brink of a blow-up to decide to take time for self. Just as you make plans to do everything else, purposely schedule in your calendar time for you. Know that self-care doesn't always require yoga and incense. It could be time at a park. It can be going to see a movie alone or treating yourself to dinner. A massage is most certainly always rejuvenating. Now that they have these Himalayan salt rooms you can sit in, try that. I hear it has many benefits for your health. If you're not claustrophobic, look into floating. It works wonders for your mind.

- ♥ If you are a single parent, self-care is a real necessity for you. I realize that child care or the lack thereof may be somewhat of a hindrance, so you have to do things a little differently if you don't have family or friends. If you do have friends, alternate amongst each other when needing a break. When I was a single mother, I used to wait until my daughter went to bed at night; I would run me a bubble bath and relax. Even married, I still do this. A bath, some candles, spa music, and wine is a free and beautiful escape. It doesn't have to be wine. It can be any beverage you have on hand. I usually use some inexpensive tea light candles. You'd be surprised at how something so simple can bring so much pleasure.

- ♥ Exercise. Yes, even exercise gives you that time alone, and I hear it's relatively healthy. Or if you play sports, use that as your exercise time and enjoy it. Like music, sports can help you escape mentally.

Whatever you choose, be mindful to self that your personal time is imperative to your inner being and those around you.

♥ ♥ ♥

Self-Love Affirmation: My family doesn't take away from my self-love.

Chapter 6

<u>Say Peace to the Past</u>

"He has redeemed my soul in peace from the battle that was against me, for there were many against me."
Psalm 55:18

D ear Self,

Please forgive me for not protecting you in every way possible. Whether it was your heart, your mind, or your body; however you needed me. I didn't realize your fragility because you've always appeared to be so strong. Instead of allowing you to seek the help you needed, I kept pushing you to go on and forcing you to keep everything bottled up inside.

The burdens that you carried, you shouldn't have had to. It was too much and way too heavy. I allowed you to lug that heaviness around for far too long. You've had to walk around in silence longer than need be. I let you blame yourself for all the things that you've gone through. Things that weren't your fault. No child should ever wonder if a man violating her body is somehow her fault. No child should be told that she should have stayed in a child's place. No child should be forced to ignore her predators when they were always right there. I should have allowed you to speak up years ago. Somebody would have listened. They would have had to. Children shouldn't have to carry the weight of someone else's demons around. That wasn't your problem to deal with or your burdens to bear.

I apologize for not speaking up about the night you were sexually assaulted. Because you had been drinking, you felt like no one would have listened. You know society has a way of placing the blame on the victims. "If she had not been doing this or doing that or dressed like this or that, it would have never happened." Their sickness was never and still isn't your fault. I was afraid of how you would be viewed. I'm so sorry.

It's not your fault that you didn't know how to communicate the traumatic events that took place in your life. You were too young to process the things that were going on. It's not your fault that you had to drag that baggage all the way into adulthood, and the same things began to happen all over again. No one can blame you for thinking that no one would believe you, had you had the strength to speak up. When you did muster up the strength to talk about bits and pieces of it, your words were brushed off, swept under a rug and, you were told, "it happens, move on." I am amazed at the number of people who told you to move on from your past traumatic events that you clearly needed to heal from. Maybe they didn't know how to help or how to listen. We've all gone through similar things, and sometimes we can't help others when we don't know how to help ourselves. So I will apologize for them as well.

I should have protected you from all the verbal abuse you've endured over the years. People don't realize how words stick with you, sometimes never to heal. Your spirit was so broken, and you didn't know how to pull yourself out of the mental hell you'd been placed in. As a child, you never received the tools needed to build up your self-esteem. There was only so much you could do. But you made it through.

Self, I've never asked your forgiveness for the harm I caused you. There was a time when I allowed you to contemplate ending it all. I never thought that you'd actually go through with it; we didn't speak on it to anyone when we should have. Then one day, out of nowhere, you decided to proceed with the thoughts you'd always had. I know it's something that you don't like to talk about, but remember lying on your bedroom floor, with some song on repeat as you waited for your sins' effects to kick in? Just a few minutes earlier, you'd taken the first steps you deemed necessary to make your life and the lives around you better. You laid there, tears rolling down your face as you drifted farther away. There were so many questions going through your mind. Yet, somehow the thought or feeling of regret wasn't one of them.

Your babies crossed your mind, but we both knew they'd be alright. At least you thought they would be. I mean, life without a mother couldn't be too bad, right? They were going to be taken care of. They had a father who was going to do everything in his power to make sure that they wouldn't want for anything. Your families would definitely step in to help. Your oldest daughter would be alright, eventually. You knew that she was going to be there for your younger brother and sister. Indeed, everything was going to be fine without you. Life would go on. It always does, right?

In the midst of all of that, you began to feel yourself drifting farther away from life. You'd truly given up. Just so you wouldn't be alone, I laid there with you.

The truth is, I was terrified. I was never taught how to protect you, so I had no training or 'wise words' to fall back on. I didn't realize your worth. I didn't know then all the amazing things you'd go on to do or the fantastic person you'd become. Besides your children, I didn't know about all the people who looked up to you. Or all the people who cared for you and needed you.

Think about it. If it hadn't been for you, if you'd succeeded in your plans, who would have helped your friend pull through in her time of need? What would have happened to your babies? Who would have gone the extra mile to help the young pregnant woman when her family had disowned her? Who would have ridden all over downtown looking for the homeless man walking in the rain with no shoes, so that he could have a pair?

I'm sure that someone would have stepped up to the plate. But you've always taken the initiative when you saw a need. You've always gone the extra mile to make others feel appreciated, loved, and needed. You are more important than you have realized. The world as a whole may not need you, but someone does. Know that from here on out, I will do all I can to protect you.

Please forgive us all.

♥ ♥ ♥

Most of us don't realize the impact that traumatic events have on us mentally until we're grown, and something triggers our memory. By traumatic, I mean anything that changes how a person thinks, feels, and views things. These experiences can range from sexual abuse to verbal abuse to neglect. Believe it or not, words or the lack thereof significantly impact us just as much as physical abuse. If a child always hears, "You're just like your mama, your daddy, etc., or you will never be (insert any negative connotation here)," and they see how these people are carrying on negatively, they won't think too highly of themselves. We begin to wonder if we should put forth the effort to be different or to change. Words that are said to us affect our self-esteem, affecting our love for self. I know you are familiar with the oft said phrase, "there's power in the tongue." There is truth to that. Words are indeed powerful.

I never thought about how much my mind needed to be protected from the thoughts I have each day. We go about our day, avoiding toxic situations because of how they make us feel or avoiding those people who I call "energy drainers" because they suck the life out of us. We must put forth that same effort when it comes to our thoughts. We wouldn't allow people to speak negative things into our lives, why should we tolerate negative language from ourselves? What you say to you matters. Words carry energy in the tone that was spoken. Remember when I said, "lower your tone when you talk to you?" It may sound funny, but I genuinely mean it.

Have you ever had someone say something in a harsh manner to you, and it feels like somebody took your heart and squeezed it? That's energy. What you speak over yourself and how you speak it greatly impacts how you view yourself. Just as you would protect yourself from others, you must protect yourself from you as well. Change your thoughts.

For a long time, I treated and talked to myself like I wasn't much. Although it's not the main reason, a fair bit of the reason had to do with what was stolen from me at a young age, my innocence. Once our innocence is stripped away from us, we can't get that back. If you've never been in a situation that's made you question anything or everything about yourself, then I take my hat off to you. You are one blessed individual, and you have so much to be grateful for because trauma can significantly impact the relationship you have with yourself. Whether it happened when you were a child or as an adult, it changes the way you view yourself.

Before an experience, you go through life, happy go lucky. After something happens, it's like you've been slapped with a ton of bricks, and now you feel like you can't trust your own judgment. So you begin to do things differently just to cope. Like a domino effect, one thing leading to another, past experiences sent me down another path, opening doors for me to experience even more things that made me question my self-worth.

Not only was I careless with my words, but I was reckless with my body. Sexing and dancing had become my coping mechanism. If no one else found value in this temple that God had given me, why would I? Toxic thinking. There were times when I sought out sex and parties to dance at just to feel as if someone loved me. I wanted to feel as if someone appreciated me. Because when I walked in a room with something super skimpy on, I was hard to ignore. I didn't have to demand the attention; it just came. Whatever false sense of security I felt the night before would all be gone the very next day because I went back to being regular old me. Someone that no one noticed or paid attention to. That didn't feel good to me. It's hard to admit, but that's probably one of many reasons I went from relationship to relationship, I wanted to feel some sense of love and belonging. I wasn't aware that I would never be filled with the love that I was seeking without loving me first. It had to come from within.

If you believe in the transference of energy and spirits as I do, you can only imagine all the junk I had to sort through and get rid of to find the love I was seeking. I was causing myself more damage and harm than anybody off the streets by allowing others to take advantage of me.

When it comes to protecting yourself, it doesn't only apply to your intimate relationships. Protecting yourself applies to family as well. I can't tell you how many times I've watched people fake and pretend at family functions because they had to interact with the uncle that violated them. Or with the mother that abandoned them. Putting on these fake smiles and doing these uncomfortable pat hugs, all the while talking yourself through the whole encounter. You know the talks we give ourselves, "it's only for a little while, just get through dinner." That's a soul-draining experience. I learned years ago, blood makes us related, but it doesn't make us family. I also learned that it's okay not to force yourself to interact with those relatives who make you feel uncomfortable. But you can forgive them for the pain they caused and keep it moving. You can pray for healing and strength. Maybe one day a relationship can be mended, but don't force yourself when you're not ready.

As I got older, I realized that my body and mind were my two most prized possessions, and I was in desperate need of change. Otherwise, I was going to continue on this never-ending cycle of self-hate, blaming others for my being stagnant and still. I had to shift my thoughts and focus.

Thankfully, my renewed faith and belief in my God gave me the strength I needed, while reminding me who I was. Just as I have to speak love into me continually, I have to regularly remind myself that I am a child of God. My mama made sure that I knew that "there was no condemnation to them which are in Christ Jesus, who walk not after the flesh, but after the Spirit, Romans 8:1." So there was nothing that I did in my past that I should be holding against myself because God wasn't holding it against me. So you, too, shouldn't allow yourself to hold your past experiences against yourself. God forgives you; therefore, you should forgive yourself. After all, He created you. He knows you. Most of all you have to remember that He loves you unconditionally. Jeremiah 31:3 tells us that God has loved us with an everlasting love. We live with ourselves every day, why not love ourselves with the same passion God has for us? Speaking from personal experiences, I know that it isn't easy. But as stubborn as people say that I am, if I can change and retrain what I think about myself, you can as well.

God used someone very close to me one Sunday. He delivered a message 'hot off the press' as I like to call those nuggets that come across the pulpit, especially when they tell you that part of the message wasn't in their notes. He said, "stop treating yourself like you're your enemy." When I tell you that one phrase shifted me again, it was just a simple reminder not to allow myself to sink back into my way of thinking. I'm here to tell you the exact same thing. You are not your enemy. You are not your past. Stop beating yourself up over something that someone said to you or did to you. Stop allowing your mind to dwell on things you can't change. Remove the self-doubt that was caused as a side effect. Accept that you aren't perfect. It has nothing to do with what uncle 'so and so' did, but everything to do with your humanness. As much as we want to be perfect and as much as we strive to be, we won't ever be. It's just the reality of it all.

Remember, your past experiences don't determine who you are and what you can do now. If you're at the very bottom, at your lowest, there is nowhere else to go but up. Lift your eyes, hold your head up, and readjust your crown. Stick your chest out if you have to. Tell yourself that you are not your past. Your words have meaning. That's where your strength lies. Your traumatic experiences may have shaken you a little bit, but you can take those pieces and put them back together just the way you want to.

I'm reminded of the art of Kintsugi. In Japanese culture, they use a unique technique to restore broken pottery. When it's broken, instead of using gorilla glue, as I do, they take those pieces and put them back together using melted gold. The idea is to get others to embrace a stronger, more powerful piece of work. It's supposed to get us to recognize just how beautiful we are with all of our flaws and imperfections. It shows the world that, "yeah, I may have been broken at one point, you can even see my scars. However, I'm still standing. I'm still beautiful. I'm stronger, and I'm still able to go on." That's an affirmation within itself. Say those last lines every day until you feel it deep down within.

♥ ♥ ♥

Self-Love Affirmation: I am at peace with my past.

Part Two:

From This Day Forward

Chapter 7

Know What Forgiveness Is

"I acknowledged my mistakes to You, and You forgave them."
Psalm 32:5

Forgiveness. The act of letting go of resentment, anger toward something, a situation, or someone. Forgiveness wasn't something that I was too keen on when I was younger. As I got older, forgiving became something even harder to do. Please don't get me started on holding a grudge. You could do something to me, go on about your day, and I would be left there brewing. I would be scheming and planning my revenge. It didn't matter how long it took. I was going to get you back, somehow or another. Some people would refer to that as being petty. That was me.

When I think back on all the times people used to tell me to smile or ask me why I was always looking so mean, it was probably because I was plotting. Have you ever seen somebody that hardly ever smiled and they looked like they were always constipated? Eyes glowered, lips tight, and they looked like their stomach hurt? If you know anything about Jeff Dunham's ventriloquist act, picture Walter. You could see it all over his face; Walter was always salty and miserable, always looking stuck up and constipated. That was me holding on to unforgiveness. Just ugly. I needed to let go of all hopes for a better past and focus on having a self-loving future.

But why was it so hard to forgive? Could it have been that I was trying to protect myself? Perhaps, I thought that holding on to grudges was my way of punishing the person I felt wronged me. Or maybe I thought that forgiving meant that I condoned the act or behavior that caused me turmoil and pain. Either way, I didn't want anyone to feel like they had the upper hand over me, so I chose to hold on; that way I'd never allow them to hurt me again.

As I got older, I learned that forgiveness was very vital to my health. Bitterness was making me sick. The more I held on to the past hurts caused by others, the more I would slip into darkness. The more I slipped, the worse I would feel. There were plenty of nights I'd wake up with chills, shivering like it's freezing in the room, and it wasn't even cold. I'd be nauseous for no reason. I'd developed ailments and would go to the doctor only to have them tell me that they couldn't find anything wrong with me. The bottom line, I was holding on to too much toxicity.

Holding on to any type of waste is pointless and exhausting. That's why a healthy body does everything it can to rid itself of waste. Imagine what holding on to past hurts does to you. It creates emotional imbalances. Holding on to things that you no longer have control over, such as the past, causes anger issues and depression. I was lashing out at people because they may have done something to trigger my past emotions. Unforgiveness was destroying me and everyone around me. I had to make a choice. I needed to let go of the pain, anger, and resentment. I needed to set myself free. It took me a while, but I figured out that if it was crucial to my health for me to forgive others, it was equally important for me to forgive myself.

The hardest thing for me to do was to let go of all the hurt and pain I brought on myself. If someone wronged me, I could easily cut ties with them and keep going. However, I couldn't just cut all ties with myself. Believe me; I've tried. I can't tell you the many days I spent loathing, filling myself with more hate for myself, kicking myself further into the ground. I was dwelling on things that I could not change.

Whew, that past is something else. It's like we have an ongoing view of all the negative stuff on replay. Let me put it to you this way. Have you ever had a relationship to end, and you find the saddest song and put it on repeat? Please don't play with me; we've all been there in some form. You play that song over and over for a few hours, a couple of days. Weeks even. Each day you'd feel worse than the day before.

How did you expect to move on from that relationship if you were sitting there, forcing yourself to listen to *Lately* by Divine all day? Forcing tears out of your eyes, thinking the messier you can look, the better you may feel. That's exactly how it is when you are replaying your past over and over again. Allow me to insert a "thank you" to God for growth and change. When I tell you that I had that feeling sorry for myself down to a tee, that would be an understatement. The same concept of letting go applies to you. Take those thoughts off of repeat.

Letting go and forgiving has so many benefits. Forgiving ourselves improves our well-being, mentally and physically. It makes us more optimistic, more positive. When we're more positive, we are more productive. We are more successful, more focused, and more loving.

Not forgiving ourselves causes us to be super critical of everything in and around us. At times, we don't even recognize that we're doing it. I know I'm always catching myself saying negative things when I do something wrong. It's the perfectionist in me, which is also a toxic trait because it means that we are keeping a running tally of our achievements somewhere deep within. If we don't achieve something, we force ourselves to believe that we've failed. Most people hate failure. Once I realized that failures are a part of life and should be viewed as lessons, my thoughts became easier to control. But holding on to that defeated way of thinking caused many self-disappointments. This led to other mental issues that I didn't need.

Then there were times I'd catch myself being judgmental and supercritical of others. I had to re-evaluate in those moments because obviously there were still some self-esteem issues within me that needed my attention.

Have you forgiven yourself?

You may be thinking, what reason would I have to forgive myself? I can think of quite a few reasons for me personally. I needed to forgive myself for all the negative thinking that I was doing and for all the negativity that

I allowed to be poured into me, criticizing my dark-skin, for thinking that my forehead was too big. Or thinking I wasn't smart enough. I'm too short. My feet were too big. I had a habit of blaming myself for things happening that were beyond my control. The list can go on. The truth of the matter is, at some point, I thought that I would never be pretty enough or good enough. Then I was introduced to Psalm 139. It says that I am fearfully and wonderfully made.

Furthermore, it says in verse fifteen that my frame wasn't hidden from God when I was being formed in secret, that I was intricately and skillfully formed [as if embroidered with many colors] in the depths of the earth. That verse alone says that much thought went into creating me. There was time and great effort put into the making of little old me. The same goes for you. God didn't skimp on you when he was creating you. He took his time with you. Okay, so what if you want to lose a few pounds or gain a couple in some cases? There's nothing wrong with that. As long as you're doing it for all the right reasons, you have every right to do those things that you feel will enhance the greatness you already encompass. After all, that too is a part of self-love.

How can you forgive yourself?

I realized there were steps to this challenging task. First of all, know that true forgiveness is intentional and deliberate. It would help if you made the conscious decision to release those feelings that have caused bitterness. Release those emotions that fog your brain, altering the way you feel about yourself. You have to release not just those things that you've done, but also those outside influences as well. Those things done by others that have caused you harm, whether they deserve your forgiveness or not, releasing them is for your own good. Then realize that:

- ♥ As adults, we have to hold ourselves accountable for the things that we've allowed to happen. Those are the things that we felt could be life-changing, but we did them anyway. If there were things that happened to us as children, then we have to accept that it happened. We can't change it. But we shouldn't dwell on them either. Also, we have to be empathetic towards our younger self and her experiences. Face those giants, seek inner healing, and push forth.

- ♥ Having empathy and compassion towards our younger beings, allows us to sort through any shame or guilt we may be feeling. However, we must not wallow in that shame and guilt. We're not bad people; we're human. Allow yourself to be present in your feelings for the moment. Then look at the things you can learn and apply them to the now.

- ♥ Reconcile the relationship that you have with yourself. Just as you would have to reconcile with those who have hurt you, or you them, you sometimes have to reconcile with yourself. As I said, you're stuck with you. According to Gandhi, Mandela, and Mother Theresa, "hatred of one's self is the worst sin man could ever commit." Tell your inner critic to be quiet, accept that you aren't perfect, and move on.

♥ ♥ ♥

Self-Love Affirmation: I forgive myself.

Chapter 8

Deal with It

"Though they stumble, they will never fall, for the Lord holds them by the hand."
Psalm 37:24

I realized that there were a lot of things keeping me from forgiving and loving myself. One of the main things I was holding on to was past mistakes. We must forgive ourselves for the mistakes that we've made.

I'm a world renowned-chef. I prepare the finest and the most scrumptious pound cakes and pies. I put together the most delectable dishes every night. That almost always consists of the same salads with a different dressing. Did you just roll your eyes? They're homemade vinaigrettes, so it should count for something. Okay, maybe I'm not a world-renowned chef in real life, but just go with me here, please. Let me be great just for a few minutes. Besides, my babies almost always give me at least eight out of ten stars. In my mind, that makes me a world-renowned chef, a home-renowned chef at the very least.

While preparing and cooking these great dinners and desserts, I can't tell you how many times I've gone to cut the meatloaf, only to have it fall apart because I'd forgotten to add eggs to hold it together. Let me not forget the time I left the sugar out of the homemade cookies. There was the time when I pulled a fully baked cake out of the oven and decorated it, only to cut it two days later and discover that the inside of the cake was a total disaster. Not just one, but two cakes were worthy of the words, "Nailed it!" One was dry as the Sahara Desert, and the other one was half overcooked and half undercooked. Only a renowned chef would be able to pull off such a beautiful feat as that one. Not to mention, these cakes were carefully transported to a function where they were to be shared with others. I was super excited about those pound cakes. I wished you could have seen the looks on our faces. My mouth hit the floor. My confidence dropped to a negative something. Although it was a simple mistake that I'd made somewhere in the preparation process, I could have easily allowed that to define my skills and given up on baking cakes. As much as we like to eat around here, messing up our food is grounds to fall out.

Then you have those mistakes that result in money being paid out, and they kind of stick with you for a while. Like the time I let the passenger side window down to throw a bottle out, only to quickly discover that it wasn't the passenger window that I let down. Instead, it was the window in the backseat. The whole passenger window shattered in slow motion under the impact of that bottle. Guess that's what I get for trying to litter. That was a real Homer Simpson moment, "DOH!" My. Mama. Was. Pissed. I beat myself up for a long time over that broken window. I kept asking myself, how could have been so stupid as to not see that it wasn't the window in the front that you let down? My mother had forgiven me, but I couldn't forgive myself. It was money that she didn't have to spend.

Furthermore, you have those life-altering mistakes (decisions). Those that stick with you for years to come. Like underestimating your capabilities, selling your dreams short, not taking a chance on that job in another city because you were afraid. Or you were trusting the wrong people with our innermost secrets and thoughts, only to have them to be shared with others unbeknownst to you. You were competing with others besides yourself or afraid to learn or failed to learn from the past. Yes, that is a thing

These are all life-altering mistakes that we make. No matter how many times you brush them off and try to move on, they always find a way to creep back in. Until you make the conscious effort to call it out and say I forgive myself for that, the remnants will always be there. I can bring it even closer to home, those mistakes can be when you turned down a job out of state making good money because your boyfriend didn't want you to leave him. That's putting your needs and happiness on the backburner, sacrificing to make someone else happy.

That was something I allowed to beat me up for a long time. Perhaps you stayed in a relationship that was no longer conducive to your well-being, and a piece of you died day by day, little by little. You listened to someone tell you that you'd never amount to anything. Nobody will ever want you because you had a child. Or you'd end up being somebody's flunky. You allowed those words to shape you for years. They molded you. They defined who were. No matter how untrue they were, you'd heard them for so long that you started to believe them. Believing someone else's words and feelings about you is probably one of the biggest mistakes of all.

That stops right now.

Why? Because forgiveness is one of the first signs of self-love. When you are able to forgive others, then you are truly able to forgive yourself, leading to a continued journey of love for yourself. Not only that, forgiveness and self- love leads to emotional healing. Our hearts and souls are freed. That waste from emotional constipation is released. You can't afford to hold on to grudges. Your health depends on your ability and execution of forgiveness. When you forgive, you allow yourself to be released from those things that caused you pain and suffering.

Choose right now, to forgive someone and yourself. Know this: forgiveness doesn't mean you have to forget. It doesn't mean that you are dismissing what someone did or said to you. You aren't automatically letting go of how someone made you feel. Forgiving someone and yourself doesn't mean that you will be instantly happy. However, it does mean that you are choosing to start your process of healing.

Forgiveness, although difficult, is one of the most significant signs of strength. It's the most courageous thing you can do. Because in all of your hurt, you have chosen to stand strong. It means that you have made a purposeful effort to cut the emotional holds and grudges that have been hanging over your head. It means that you choose to put an end to the headaches, the nightmares, the chills. It means that you are choosing to heal.

Ways to forgive and heal are quite simple but will take time. First things first:

- ♥ We must take accountability for what we have done. When we take responsibility for our actions and acknowledge their aftereffects, self-forgiveness and growth begins.

- ♥ Discern why you did what you did. You know, those things that are causing you to feel guilt and shame. Perhaps we were trying to meet a need. If we were to think back on our past mistakes, we will probably see and understand that what we did was because it was the best that we knew how to do.

- ♥ In figuring out why we did something and seeking what to do differently, this leads to learning from our mistakes. We must ask ourselves, what did this mistake teach me? Did it lead to me being a better person?

- ♥ Then we must do the very thing that I have been doing throughout this book, we must apologize. We must ask ourselves for forgiveness. Just as we would make amends with others, say to yourself, "I'm sorry for hurting you."

- Lastly, we must remember to be mindful. In learning from our past mistakes, there is something we must do, focus, not on the error, but on the lesson learned. Then we have to actively practice, put to use the understanding we've gained.

If we continue to hold on and not release our mistakes, we will continue to walk a continuous circle of shame and guilt. We will continue to look in the mirror and see a disappointing reflection haunting us, with no good benefits to come. Don't force yourself to remain stuck when you can experience so much joy and freedom in letting go of your mistakes. Let go of that which does not define who you are. Live. Love. Be Free.

♥ ♥ ♥

Self-Love Affirmation: I am not my mistakes.

Chapter 9

No Validation Needed

"So God created man in his own image..."
Genesis 1:27

I once knew this young woman who would always go above and beyond to accomplish tasks with perfection. She'd always drive herself into madness, trying to make sure that everything was done with no flaws. When people would point out things they'd change about whatever it was she'd done, she'd become upset, defensive, and shut down. Instead of making the recommended changes, she'd go and tear apart everything she'd created because she didn't receive the accolades she'd wanted. She didn't know how to accept criticism well. She took everything very personally. As if it was a dig at her talents and hard work.

There was no doubt that she'd always compared herself to others, wondering if she was as good as the people she came in contact with. Or even on a job, when she went overboard to please her boss and clients, but no one seemed to notice. Or in school when she worked super hard to produce excellent grades, only to have no one acknowledge, but instead hone in on the lower grades and ask why. She took offense to it all.

Why did she feel this way?

She needed that validation, but instead, perceived rejection destroyed her to her very core. For some of us, invalidation begins at a young age. We need recognition and affirmation as children. We need approval from our parents. We desire confirmation that what we do is good, and when we don't get it, we question our self-worth, and our self-esteem begins to dwindle. Feelings of invalidation, more times than not, carry over into adulthood. If we don't learn that our self-worth isn't dependent upon others' opinions or views of us, we will become vulnerable to manipulation, allowing others to define us.

A person such as this, lives in constant need of approval. I know because I lived in a constant need for approval. If someone told me that I was great, then guess what, I was great. If, heaven forbid, they said to me that I was bad, then that's just what I was, and everything goes wrong from there on out. The lack of approval created a spirit of defeat within me.

Experiencing invalidation and rejection at a young age causes one to chase acceptance from others. When they don't get that which they seek, they retreat, forcing them to pull away from everyone, becoming anti-social.

Whereas in others, it causes them to become people-pleasers because they are afraid to be who they are. Not wanting to let others down, they risk their own uniqueness and sense of self. They take on all the characteristics of whomever they are hanging around at the time. If their circle of friends is always changing, then they are continually changing. Some people would call this evolving, but if you get to the core of it all, these people are actually afraid of rejection and abandonment. This creates what I call chameleons. They are the ones who blend into every environment they are introduced to. At one time or another, both of these types of people were me.

Seeking validation from others determined how I operated from day to day. Of course, I didn't realize it then, but the lack of validation created anxiety and the fear. As a result, these two emotions kept me from trying things I knew I'd like to keep the focus from being on me. Or to keep from being questioned about my choices. It caused me to turn down opportunities in fear of performing poorly or failing at whatever I did. Lack of validation and rejection caused me to surround myself with internal darkness and block everything and everyone out.

Because I lacked the approval of others, I didn't understand my own value. I didn't know my worth. This misunderstanding affected my love for self tremendously. I had to learn how to look within. Because it wasn't what I did, it was who I was. I was a beauty created by God himself. He knew my name. He knows the number of hairs on my head. He knows when circumstances are going to cause me to question myself. He even knows when I'm going to show all the way out, forgetting who I am. However, He is constantly reminding me that my value does not lie within man. It doesn't lie in my accomplishments or my job nor my children. But my value lies deep within God.

Your value, self-worth, and self-esteem come from within you. Once you begin the process of healing and acceptance for self, you can start to grow and thrive. You can begin to fall in love with yourself. You will be able to look in the mirror and smile at the woman smiling back at you.

You can do this by becoming your own measuring scale. Don't depend on others to lift you up. Don't compare yourself to others. You are in competition with no one. The only person you should be striving to surpass, is the person you were yesterday. The only person who can define you is you. Know your strengths, focus on them. You are no longer that powerless child that sought the approval of her parents or her friends. You are that powerful woman who is worth far more than rubies and diamonds. You have been equipped with gifts, talents, and strengths. You are validated by God.

❤ ❤ ❤

Self-Love Affirmation: I compete with no one.

Chapter 10

Know Yourself

*"I am the vine; you are the branches.
If you remain in me and I in you, you will bear much fruit…"*
John 15:5

There is a famous phrase that we've all heard some time or another in our lives. I will be honest and admit that for a long time, I thought it was scripture. For some, it may have been. The phrase or maxim, as it is called, "Know thyself" has been an often-used statement in philosophy. It seems simple. However, anybody that's taken any kind of class dealing with philosophy and psychology knows that you have to think beyond what you think you already know. Deep, isn't it? The phrase has been attributed to many ancient Greeks and taken on different meanings throughout history. However, in a nutshell, I believe that the base meaning remains the same: to have knowledge of self. When you know who you are deep within, you know your capabilities and limitations.

Discovering who you are is a lifelong process. I've even heard someone say that it takes a life-time for someone to know themselves. This thought alone is one of the reasons I try my best to refrain from using the phrases, "that'll never be me" or "I'd never do anything like that." As a matter of fact, I try my best not to say what I would and wouldn't do because I never know what any situation in life will bring out of me. There have been some things that I've gone through and dealt with that left me saying, "Wow! I didn't know I had that in me!"

As I stated earlier, we are all constantly evolving. With each passing season and circumstance in your life, you have to continue to find you. Good or bad, every situation that we deal with is shaping us. We are constantly becoming who we are meant to be; our interests are forever changing. Even our temperaments vary throughout our lives; therefore, it will take your entire life to know exactly who you are.

I told you, for a long time, I didn't know who I was. I never took the time to get to know me because I was always so wrapped up in others and doing things to make them happy. It wasn't until I'd gotten so lost and confused, depressed and down, tired of being tired, that I decided to pay attention to Tracie. I began to study myself, and I made up my mind to focus on me. I begin to learn different tools and apply them to my life, in return, re-establishing my self-love. Now, if I ever have to step foot in another therapist's office, I will be able to answer the questions, "Who are you?" and "What makes you, you?" I can tell them, and whoever else wants to know, that I am a woman of God. I am fully capable of doing anything I put my mind to. I am a Queen.

I enjoy sitting in the park, listening to nature, and the laughter of children. I love the natural elements presented by the earth. I marvel at the double rainbows after the rain; I become engulfed in the smell of wet grass. I find peace in the gray skies after a thunderstorm. I get lost in abstract art. I'm not crazy, but I love crime shows. I love the mysterious and the unknown. I find solace in coloring. Most importantly, I believe unicorns exist. Although this is nowhere near an extensive list of what makes me who I am, I can finally tell you something, and it's the total truth. I can finally breathe, and with each breath I take, I love me more.

You, too, can speak confidently in knowing yourself. It takes time and effort, but it is possible. It is a must. Take a moment and think about those things that are important to you. What do you believe in? What motivates you? Besides yourself, what do you value? You may not be able to answer those questions right off but think about them. Once you have that figured out, you can begin to build on knowing yourself.

Think about your hobbies, those things that you find pleasure in. What is something that you can get lost in and not realize that time is passing you by? For me, it's a good book. Reading will transport me out of this world, and the next thing I know, I'm besties with characters and will get an attitude because I've never learned how to "read in moderation." At least I get my money's worth.

Whatever it is that has the power to draw you in and hold you for a while, and it brings you positive pleasure that propels you to become your best self, nurture it. Who knows, that passion could lead to deep pockets if you know what I mean.

Remember your feelings and how you deal with things. When you know this, you can know which situations to avoid, making you doubt yourself. For instance, I'm an introvert. I've always been an introvert, and I don't anticipate that changing. Now, don't get me wrong, I can tolerate being in spaces with a lot of people, but I have to be mindful of my emotions and know when enough is enough.

Knowing your personality and traits is vital to understanding yourself.

Be mindful of your day to day activities. Recognize when you are at your best and operate at full capacity in that moment. Have you ever heard about people that say they can't sleep past a particular hour, and when they do, they feel like their whole day is gone because they woke up five minutes later than usual? Those people, first of all, are weird. I'm just joking. Laugh a little. Those people are in tune with their biological clocks. They are the ones that don't mind saying no and are good at negotiating their time. Moment of truth, I haven't quite mastered that yet. Remember, I'm a work in progress.

Set goals for yourself. Think about things that you want to accomplish and why you want to achieve them. These goals could be something that you enjoyed doing in the past and can quite often lead you on a new path to prosperity and success. Sit down and think about some of those situations that have happened in your life; it could be anything. Preferably something positive. Hone in on how they made you feel and see if you can change those meaningful events into a goal.

I asked my mama once what made her decide to sit with people. She said that she saw the toll it took on her family when the elders got sick. Her sister and cousin had to handle things by themselves. She wanted to bring relief to other families, so they wouldn't have to stress and worry about whether or not their loved ones were in good hands. I asked her if sitting with people shaped her into becoming a better version of herself. With so much satisfaction, she simply replied, "Absolutely." What she does is gratifying to her. She used her compassion to accomplish a mission, not just for herself, but for others. My mama is a firm believer in "you reap what you sow." She knows that what she puts out into the atmosphere will come back. Therefore, she's not concerned about the type of treatment she'll receive when it's her time to be catered to. Only a woman who has a real sense of self knows how to live by such valuable words.

People who truly know themselves also know their abilities and they know their characteristics. Knowing these things, they know what makes them powerful. They know what sets them apart from everyone else. This doesn't mean that no one else can have the same traits and characteristics as them, but they know that there's only one of them, and they bring their own unique quirkiness to the world.

Being confident in who you are brings so many rewards. My greatest reward in knowing myself is my happiness. Before, I felt as if my inner being, my inner thoughts were always cloudy. Sometimes it even hurt to think about myself when someone asked, "who are you?" Now there is so much joy in me. My spirit is at peace, and I feel a thousand pounds lighter. When you know who you are, you're more tolerable, and you have better control of yourself.

Control happens because you recognize what makes you tick, allowing you to walk away from those situations that throw you off balance. Knowing yourself also allows you to stay grounded in your truth and what's important to you. You begin to learn how to say no to those things that aren't beneficial to your growth on this continuous self-love journey.

The other greatest asset of knowing oneself, is that the conflicts you have within yourself begin to diminish with each passing experience. You will probably second guess yourself from time to time, but you will start to be more confident than before. I mean, I still have moments where I don't know if I want chocolate ice cream or butterscotch. So I just get both. I understand that this throws that whole self-control point out the window. Say it with me, "work in progress."

No matter what it takes or how long it takes for you to fall in love with who you are if you don't remember anything that's been said before, remember this: Be true to yourself.

♥ ♥ ♥

Self-Love Affirmation: I know who I am.

Chapter 11

Thank Yourself

"But blessed is the one who trusts in the Lord, whose confidence is in him."
Jeremiah 17:7

Dear Self,

Thank you.

Thank you for not completely giving up and throwing in the towel. Thank you for standing tall and strong even when you felt like you were at your weakest. When all you could do at times was cry, you still held on. Although you got a late start due to missteps, thank you for being the first one in your family to graduate college. When you could have given up after failing the GRE, you decided to take the MAT, hence graduating from college with your Master's.

Thank you for not allowing your fear of flying to overpower your desire to see new places. You had an absolute ball in Hawaii and the Dominican Republic. Girl, your taste buds can't thank you enough for the good food you pigged out on. The clear blue waters and soft sands you felt between your toes can't be matched to any other. At least not right now. But I promise you, we will top it somehow.

Thank you for not giving up on all of your dreams. No matter how many doors were closed in your face. No matter how many jobs told you that you were under-qualified or lacked experience. No matter how many rejection notices you received, you kept on going. Using your creativeness, you always found a way. Girl, you are a boss in your own right.

Thank you for being open and vulnerable, no matter how many times you've been let down. You had every reason to shut completely down, but you chose to fight. Because for some reason, giving up has never been an option for you. When you felt like all hope was gone, you kept moving forward. Baby, I admire your tenacity.

When you didn't think you'd make it, you trudged on. When you saw no end in sight, you kept going through the darkness. Even with all the messed up choices you've made in life, they molded and shaped you into the beautiful, strong woman you are today. When your best didn't seem good enough, thank you for still trying and giving it your all.

Thank you for your transparency and not being afraid to admit that sometimes you were scared as hell. Thank you for crying in the wee hours of the morning. I've always felt that tears cleansed the soul. Thank you for accepting that you aren't perfect, and it's okay to fail. Thank you for learning from your mistakes.

Thank you for having sense enough to know that you can't live this life on your own. Thank you for your renewed faith and belief that God will see you through it all. Thank you for being weak. For you realized that when you were weak, God was strong, and he carried you. He is still carrying you. Thank you for learning how to allow the negativity to roll off like water on a duck's back.

Thank you for being unbothered and learning how to be authentically you.

Here's to more joyous experiences, more moments of self-love, and leaving your trace around this world.

I love you so much.
Tracie ♥

♥ ♥ ♥

Seeking self-love is an ongoing journey. While on this journey, there are a few things that we must remember:

- ♥ Be intentional.
    - o Remember that YOU are the only person responsible for how you feel about yourself. No one has the power to make you feel guilty or doubt who you are. Release yourself from self-blame and shame. Acceptance of self is far more rewarding than hating.

- ♥ Celebrate.
    - o Celebrate your small wins along the way. Celebrate your strengths. It's natural for us to condemn ourselves when we fall. But congratulate yourself for being able to get back up. You'd be surprised how great it feels to pat yourself on the back every now and again. And smile. You've overcome so much in life, turn up one time for that. Don't count yourself out.

- ♥ Be aware of the people around you.
    - o If you ever feel drained when you hang around certain people, re-evaluate that circle. Be cognizant of the tone and nature of the conversations you're having with

the people around you. Ask yourself: Are there negative connotations being tossed around? What are the people around me speaking into my life? Even in a jokingly manner, words take root. Not does words take roots, but spirits travel. If you are drained after a simple lunch with friends, distance yourself from them. Surround yourself with people who live in a positive light and have the ability to lift you up. After all, we have a tendency to take on the characteristics of those we are around.

- ♥ Tell your inner critic to shut up.
    - o Listen, I don't know about you, but sometimes it feels good for me to tell someone to shut up. Okay, I know it's rude to tell someone to shut up, but there are times when they just need to hear it. Know what I mean? Your inner critic needs to hear it. Sometimes your inner critic can be very judgmental of you and makes you feel worse than you already do. So that you're not being rude to yourself, you can pleasantly say, "shhhhhh, I got it from here."

- ♥ Bury the past.

- o When we come to grips that we can't change our past, we can be better accepting and move on through the now. Whether they were mistakes that we've made, things that have happened to us, or dreams deferred. We can't do anything about it. Let it go and keep your eyes on your future.

♥ Be nice to yourself.
- o Realize that in you being nice to yourself, you are also being understanding of your inner being. Love you for you, flaws and all. Recognize that you don't have it all together, and you never will. Remember that you aren't the only one in this world who doesn't have it all together.

♥ Surrender.
- o All negative thoughts that you have about yourself, let it go. We, as humans, are changing and evolving, hopefully into better versions of ourselves. Because of that, we are not who we used to be. There's a saying that a different version of you exists in the minds of everyone you know. None of those versions matter except the version you have of yourself. Since

we become what we think, why not think of you being your best self, even if at that moment you aren't. One day you will be. But the journey to that person starts right now.

- ♥ Live, Love, and Be FREE!!
    - o Live your life to the fullest extent possible. Don't allow anyone to judge you on how you style your hair, do your makeup, or how you dress. For all these things showcase how you feel about you. Your love for self seeps through your pores. It oozes out of your, making you glisten like the ocean under the moon. Why do you think people glow when they're happy?
    - o Love yourself unconditionally. Don't allow anyone to make you feel that loving yourself is selfish. Loving you enables you to love others, even when they don't deserve it.
    - o Being free allows you to remove societal shackles that have been placed on you for years. Don't force yourself to live in a size five mold when you were clearly created with a size twelve attitude. With all of your being remember to live authentically true to you.

- ♥ Thank yourself.
    - o Gratitude is about being thankful. All the things that you do for others to show your appreciation, you can also do for self. Write yourself a "Thank You" letter. Buy yourself flowers. Treat yourself to a spa day. Live in the now.

- ♥ Trust God.
    - o I intentionally left this last because I feel that it is the most important. Trust your designer, your creator. No one defines who you are, but God. Lean into him, and he will give you a clear vision of who you are. You, beautiful, are the apple of his eye.

♥ ♥ ♥

Self-Love Affirmation: I love me.

Epilogue

"She is clothed with strength and dignity, and she laughs without fear of the future."
Proverbs 31:25

If you've been paying close attention to each chapter's end, you would have noticed that each one ended with an affirmation. Affirmations are powerful, positive statements that will challenge and change you if you allow them. Affirmations provide us with the energy we need to overcome negativity, opening us up to the reality we desire. The key to affirmations is that they have to be repeated until they have been engraved in your thoughts. Positive affirmations have the power to take charge, holding our negative thoughts hostage. After they have been engraved, continue to repeat them until you begin to believe in what you are saying. You will begin to notice your behavior and attitude change. Your thoughts will become more positive. You will feel revived.

There will be days when you don't feel like being positive or when you don't feel as if the affirmations are worth saying. Those are the days you should say them most. You have to keep going until you feel that your mind has been reprogrammed. Be patient with yourself because change does not happen overnight. Reprogramming takes time. When you repeat daily affirmations, there are a few things you need to keep in mind. It doesn't matter what time of day it is; you can stop and affirm wherever you are. You can pause for a moment, affirm, and keep going. You can say affirmations in the morning, before getting your day started. Mornings are usually the best time, as positive thoughts set the tone for the rest of your day. Then you can give yourself small reminders throughout the day.

I don't want to leave you hanging, so I will provide you with some tips, as well as remind you of the affirmations to get you started.

- ♥ Look in the mirror.
    - o If you're home, stand in front of the bathroom mirror. If you're in your car and parked, use the rearview mirror. Invest in an inexpensive handheld mirror for those on the go moments.
    - o Look into your eyes and smile.

- ♥ Remember to breathe.
    - o Think about the breathing exercise I mentioned earlier. Inhale positivity through your nose. Then exhale

negativity through your mouth. Do this for thirty seconds, breaking it up into ten-second sections.

- ♥ Repeat any affirmation that you are feeling the need to. Allow yourself to focus on each word and how they make you feel.
- ♥ Absorb.
    - o Take in every positive feeling and emotion, allowing those feelings to wrap you in a warm embrace.

♥ ♥ ♥

Self-Love Affirmations

- ♥ I love me and all that I am.
- ♥ I am beautiful.
- ♥ I am a human work in progress.
- ♥ I am lovable.
- ♥ I am loved.
- ♥ I love myself.
- ♥ I am more than enough.
- ♥ My family doesn't take away from my love for self.
- ♥ I am at peace with my past.
- ♥ I forgive myself.
- ♥ I am not my mistakes.
- ♥ I compete with no one.
- ♥ I know who I am.

This is nowhere near an exhaustive list of affirmations. As your love for yourself grows, you can create your own affirmations to write down or say each day.

I want to leave you with a quote by Daniel Defoe, "The soul is placed in the body like a rough diamond, and must be polished, or the luster of it will never appear."

We can learn so much from the production of diamonds. They are symbolic of light and life. Diamonds are presented as emblems of purity, invincibility, and power. Diamonds are unconquerable. They are one of the most admired stones because of their ability to survive a difficult journey. Diamonds are strong.

Most of us have only seen the finished product of such a beautiful jewel. We get lost in the carat or the weight of the diamond. We marvel at the color, clarity, and cut. We rarely think about what it takes to develop a diamond. Instead, we often think, "The bigger, the better." However, size shouldn't matter because all authentic diamonds go through the same beating and shaking. Big or small, size doesn't determine a diamond's true value. Only the exact process does.

Before the fire and polishing, a diamond is formed in what is known as kimberlite, which looks like a deep hole of worn rock. In this deep hole, you will find carbon, a black, elemental compound. To the naked eye, one may not recognize that they've stumbled upon a pit full of value and wonder, simply because of its dull, yellowish-brown, or black rocks. In its rare state, a diamond serves no purpose. It could be worn, but people may look and wonder why you're walking around with a rock on. In order to be appreciated, it must go through a process. The diamond has to be unearthed, removed from its darkened state. Once it has been removed, the diamond, in its natural form, is then cut. All the impurities have to be chipped away. Then it has to be shaped and polished. Of course, this isn't the extensive process of how carbon becomes a diamond; but see yourself as the diamond you are or becoming.

In order to fulfill your purpose, you must allow your "kimberlite" to be explored. You must be plucked out of your darkness. Your outer shell has to be chipped away so that a beautiful soul can be revealed. To do this, you have to gain awareness of who you are. After gaining understanding, chip at the layers. Just as a diamond isn't formed and polished overnight, expect your greatness to take time. Breaking habits takes time. Ridding your mind of negative thoughts takes time. Becoming rounded takes time. In this process, one thing you must never do is give up. You may grow weary, but never stop digging for your inner diamond. Never stop chipping. Keep polishing. Never forget that you survived a difficult journey, and you deserve to shine.

You are strong. You are in invincible. You are peace and love. Everything that you've ever gone through or experienced has prepared you for your future. Take a long, hard look in the mirror. If you must, ask yourself, "Who am I?" With great affirmation, tell yourself that you are an attractor of love, strength, power, and courage. You house harmony, creativity, endurance, and faith. You are fearfully and wonderfully made. You are the apple of God's eye. You are the embodiment of self-love. Remind yourself of this daily. Most importantly, don't forget to remind every woman you come in contact with that they too, are diamonds.

I see you. I love you.